Coffers, Clysters, Comfrey and Coifs

the lives of our seventeenth century ancestors

Janet Few

The Family History Partnership

Published by
The Family History Partnership
57 Bury New Road
Ramsbottom, Bury
Lancashire BL0 0BZ

ISBN: 978 1 906280 33 8

First Published 2012

Printed and bound by
Information Press, Southfield Road
Eynsham, Oxford OX29 4JB

Our seventeenth century ancestors may be people that we can identify, or they may be lurking, nameless, waiting to be discovered. In either case they existed, therefore we owe it to them to find out more about their way of life. This book sets out to provide an all-important context for these ancestors, ancestors whose detailed biographies probably elude us.

Acknowledgements

Martha Barnard, Robert Barnard, Chris Braund, Graeme Leese, Rebecca Leese, the staff, past and present, at Torrington 1646 <<**www.torrington-1646.co.uk**>>

Some of the material in this book first appeared in articles by Janet Few, that were published in Family Tree Magazine, <<**www.family-tree.co.uk**>>

Contents

CHAPTER 1

Truckle Beds, Tapestries, Trenchers and Thatch: homes and furnishings

House and Home

If we could open the doors of the homes of our Stuart ancestors, what would we find? Unfortunately, unless we descend from the lords of the manor, the houses that survive have been modernised and gentrified. Today's character cottages, now retailing for extortionate sums, would be unrecognisable to those who lived there in the 1600s. Let us then, peel back the layers of time and try to understand how and where, our seventeenth century forebears lived.

Only the wealthy could afford to transport building supplies, so labourers built their homes from materials that were available locally. This meant that housing styles varied with the regional geology; the granite cottages of Cornwall giving way to the cob[1] walls of Devon, for example. What was known as cob in Devon, was dob in Hampshire and dabbins or daubins in Cumberland. Brick walls were almost unheard of in the homes of ordinary families.

Roofs too depended on what could be accessed easily and for the most part, were thatched. Thatch was formed of a perma-

Cob was made from mud, horse or cow dung, straw and rubble.

nent under-coat, normally of bracken and a top, or weathering, coat of wheat straw. Varieties of wheat, in the seventeenth century, had stems that could be four or five feet long. These were ideal both for thatching and also for making rope. The Stuarts were aware that thatch came with inherent fire risks and some towns banned it for this reason.[2] When London was rebuilt, after the Great Fire of 1666, thatch was not

---

1 Cob was made from mud, horse or cow dung, straw and rubble. The thick walls would be compacted together and white washed.
2 For example, Litchfield banned thatched roofs in 1690.

Where houses be reeded (as houses have need)
Now pare off the mosse, and go beat in the reed:
The juster ye drive it, the smoother and plaine,
More handsome ye make it, to shut off the raine

From Thomas Tusser's *500 Points of Husbandry*

allowed. Where buildings were tightly packed, thatch might be covered with a layer of plaster as a fire deterrent. Brick built chimneys were a social revolution, reducing fire risk and changing cooking methods; by the seventeenth century they were found in most dwellings.

The window, or wind-eye, was where the wind got in. Originally, the move away from solid walls was in order to let light in and smoke out. Medieval windows did not open but in Tudor times, casements were more popular and sash windows were found in middle and upper class housing by the late 1600s. Windows were not necessarily glazed. The poorest might cover the gap in their wall with sacking or it might be filled with horn or with linen steeped in linseed oil to increase transparency. Wooden shutters were common and proved an effective method of keeping out the cold and rain but as they also kept out the light, they rather defeated the object. Curtains were not used at windows until the eighteenth century.

Glass windows were only present in high status housing. The use of glass developed from ecclesiastical architecture and the glass may have been amber or green, rather than clear. Such was the value of window glass, that it was not unusual to take it with you when moving house. Although blown glass had been produced in Roman times, panes of glass were still difficult to manufacture. They remained small in size and were often imported from Italy. Lead strips were used to hold the panes

The Inventory of John Paddon of Winkleigh 1657

Hall - Table board, form, little cupboard,
    dressing board, chairs and stools
Parlour - Bedstead, 2 chests, 2 coffers, chair,
    truckle bed, dust bed
Hall Chamber - Bedstead, truckle bed, table
    board, form, 2 coffers, 8 spoons
Parlour Chamber - Bedstead, dust bed
Men's Chamber - 2 bedsteads and dust beds

in place, often so that they formed a diamond pattern. It has been suggested that contemporary writers found the use of glass to be widespread,[3] this is hyperbole and it was not until the late eighteenth century that window glass was commonly found in labouring homes. As windows, glazed or not, were regarded as a necessity they were a prime candidate for taxation. The window tax, introduced in 1696, was looked upon as a tax on daylight, hence the expression, 'daylight robbery'. Even when the tax was brought in, there were only eighteen manufacturers of window glass in England and Wales, most of whom were based in London or Bristol.

Andrew Boorde's '*Dyetary of Health*', written in 1542, described the ideal situation for a home. 'The air must be pure, frisky and clean; the foundations of gravel mixed with clay. The chief prospects should be east and west, or north-east and south-west; never south for the south wind doth corrupt and make evil vapours'. Attempts were made to avoid high winds but damp was seen as a necessary evil. In fact, mud based walls deteriorated in dry conditions. Most ordinary homes still had compacted mud floors. More substantial dwellings would have stone flags or tiles and by the end of the century, floor boarding was more common. Carpets were rare. Although they are more often associated with the nineteenth century, some Stuart housewives would tear old textiles into strips, which would be pushed through hessian, using a prodder and tied to form a rag-rug.

Inventories sometimes give an indication of the different rooms in seventeenth century dwellings however the homes of the poorest sections of society are not represented here. Most cottages of the time had two stories, although the upper floor may have been under the eaves and accessed only by a ladder. Older farmhouses often had stone spiral staircases, usually winding round the chimney stack. Properties built in the seventeenth century were more likely to have wooden stairs. Downstairs would be the living room, in the literal sense of the word. Here day to day living and cooking took place. The room often doubled as sleeping quarters for some members of the family.

---

3   Davies, Godfrey. *The Early Stuarts 1603-1660* 1959, Oxford University Press, p. 386, referring to the 1671 writings of John Aubrey.

Although many farmers still lived in dwellings that had their origins in the hall house or longhouse, in the 1600s, livestock tended to have their own accommodation. There might have been part of the ground floor that was partitioned off for the messy jobs and this may still have been used to house animals in bad weather. This area was to develop into the scullery and later the utility room. Upstairs would be a bedroom for the parents and youngest children, with the older children sleeping together behind a curtain or, in more sophisticated homes, a dividing wall. There was nothing that resembled the modern hall or landing and rooms normally led off one another.

Richer households may have had a closet, which was an area where adults could escape from the bustle of family life, rather than being used for activities

Older farmhouses often had stone staircases.

associated with personal hygiene. Any bathing, a rare occurrence, would take place in front of the kitchen fire. Toilet facilities were sited away from the cottage, in the privy. In towns it was normal to share this with other households and even family privies allowed for more than one occupant at a time. Chamber pots, or similar receptacles, were vital, as urine was a valued commodity with many uses and needed to be saved.

Furniture

Unless one was rich, furnishings were minimal, functional and wooden, primarily made from oak. More elaborate furniture was introduced after the Restoration when, in wealthy households, it might be embellished with veneers, lacquers or inlays. Walnut and mahogany began to replace oak as the wood of choice. More lavish items, such as mirrors and clocks appeared in grander homes. Other luxuries included paintings and tapestries. Wooden wall panelling was also for the better off. An increasingly literate middle class might possess writing desks and bookcases.

Wooden wall panelling was for the better off.

Four poster or tester beds[4] with hangings were for the well off but most families would have had some form of bed frame. The hollow wooden rectangle would be criss-crossed with thick cord, to form a mesh that supported the mattress. This worked best when the cords were firmly strung, enabling the occupant to 'sleep tight'. The mattress would be linen, stuffed with feathers, for those who could afford luxury. Flock, waste wool that was unsuitable for spinning, was the next best thing. For the poorest, sacking was filled with straw, bracken or heather, which needed changing more frequently. As the name suggests, the herb lady's bedstraw might be added to the stuffing as it smelt sweet and deterred insects. Wormwood got rid of bed bugs and camomile or lavender was used to aid sleep. Hot bricks or stones were utilised as hot water bottles. Bedding, for ordinary folk, consisted of woollen blankets and was unlikely to include linen. Truckle beds could be hidden under the main bed frame and pulled out at night. This saved space in crowded households. Those who slept on mattresses, or dust beds,[5] alone would be able to roll their bed out of the way for daytime activities.

---

4 A tester bed supported the hangings with a solid headboard and canopy, rather than the poles of a four-poster.

5 Also known as a chaff bed.

Following the French fashion, wardrobes, or armoires, began to enter wealthy households towards the end of the seventeenth century. Chests of drawers date from the mid 1660s however these refinements were rare. It was much more likely that the upper and middle classes would store clothes flat, on shelves in a linen cupboard. Ordinary folk kept their few items of spare clothing in a coffer, or chest. For the very poorest, even this was not necessary, as a peg on the wall would suffice. Most clothing was woollen, so herbs such as camphor or pennyroyal would be used to deter moths. Lavender might be put with linen clothing to make it smell pleasant.

The Inventory of Mary Braund of Barnstaple 1658

Great cedar chest
Cedar table board
6 joint stools
Nest of boxes
6 silver spoons
Escritoire
4 maps
Pictures
Looking glass
2 voiders

Camphor would be used to deter moths.

Until the latter part of the seventeenth century, seating was not upholstered. Although, by the 1680s, the upper classes might have padded armchairs, most of our ancestors sat on stools or benches. Even chairs with backs were rare in labouring households. Farmhouses might have a high backed, curved, wooden settle, which was usually sited near the fire but normally, forms would be put against the wall to provide support for the back. Much of this furniture was home made and the man of the house would be expected to have the tools and basic joinery skills required to produce simple furniture. Iron nails were not necessary. Joint stools, which feature in wills and inventories of the period, were, quite literally, jointed together with mortice and tenon joints and then secured with wooden pegs.

Tables usually came in sections, the trestle legs being separate from the table board, or flat top section. The most important member of the household might sit on a chair, rather than a stool and be in the prime position at the board; hence 'chairman of the board'. Possessions were few and far between and were mostly tools or associated with the preparation and serving of food. Often, shelving was sufficient for storage. Livery cupboards were open-shelved dressers, used to accommodate dishes and serve food. Whereas an aumbrey was a

Much of the furniture was home made.

closed cupboard, where the housewife would store her preserves and other prepared foodstuffs. For those who had items worthy of display, a court cupboard combined open shelves and a closed section.

Household Items

The cauldron, or cooking pot, was vital. This item had a variety of regional names, such as kettle, cawthern or crock. Other fireside items were also important. The iron andirons, or fire-dogs, supported the logs and might have uprights to hold a roasting spit or cooking pot. The higher the social status, the more sophisticated and varied the cooking vessels became. A chafing dish, for example, might be used for simmering. This could be placed on a small, enclosed brazier, or chafer and taken to the table to keep food warm if required.

A nef would be taken by each guest when invited out to dine.

The wealthy would eat from pewter, or even silver, dishes. A full garnish of pewter ranged from larger serving chargers down to small plates. A cutlery set, known as a nef, would be taken by each guest when invited out to dine. These did not include a fork. The two-pronged fourchette began to arrive from the continent after the Restoration. Before the advent of carving forks, meat was grasped in the left hand, using a paper wrapping as protection and carved with the right. The well-to-do used linen napkins. Customarily, these were twenty eight inches wide; this was the full width of the loom.

Heavily glazed, earthenware dishes, or tigs, might be used. The Puritan influence led to morally improving slogans appearing on such tableware. Further down the social scale, circular wooden plates, ideally made from sycamore, were beginning to replace square wooden trenchers. The latter had a small indentation for salt and gave rise to the expression 'a square meal'. Those who could afford a wooden trencher, as opposed to eating off four day old trencher bread, would not normally have starved, even if their diet lacked variety.

The square wooden trencher gave rise to the expression a 'square meal'.

Drinking vessels also varied with social status. Most ordinary families made their own, using materials that were available to them. The poor lacked time so something that was quick to make and would not need replacing, was ideal. Wooden drinking mugs came into this category. Those made from leather or horn could also be home produced. Horn can be moulded when hot, so a flat section could be formed, for attaching to the hollow tube that remained when the horn's point had been removed. These then needed gluing together, using glue that had also been home made. Leather drinking vessels had the bottoms sewn to the sides with strong thread. To prevent the beverage leaking through the holes made by the stitching, it would be lined with bitumen. Given that part of the tanning process involved soaking the hide in urine, this conjures a less than healthy image.

Glazed, earthenware mugs were often highly decorated. The family may have made these themselves or bought them in. As they were breakable, these were not for the lowest ranks of society. Only the higher classes could afford to drink from something that needed to be made by a specialist; this included pewter, silver and glass vessels.

Baskets, buckets, barrels and other storage receptacles were essential. Lanterns, holders for rush lights or candle sticks, trimmers and snuffers were also necessary. As expected, in lesser households, these would be fewer in number and poorer in quality. Items relating to leisure activities, such as books and musical instruments, on the other hand, were unknown to most families.

The majority of household goods in the homes of our ancestors were required by the housewife in the carrying out of her domestic responsibilities. It is to those many and varied tasks that we now turn, as we try to envisage how our female forebears would have spent their time, within the setting that we have just revealed.

Further Reading

Cook, Olive. *English Cottages and Farmhouses,* 1982, Thames and Hudson Ltd.

Mc Govern, Una. *Lost Crafts: rediscovering traditional skills,* 2008, Chambers.

Mercer, Eric. *English Vernacular Houses: a study of traditional farmhouses and cottages,* 1979, HMSO.

Raymond, Stuart A. *Words from Wills and other Probate Records 1500-1800: a glossary,* 2004, Federation of Family History Societies.

<<http://www.oldandinteresting.com/default.aspx>> A history of domestic paraphernalia.

CHAPTER 2

Besoms, Battledores, Butter and Bees: household tasks

It is more difficult to chronicle the day-to-day duties of the men in Stuart times, as their occupations varied. Seventeenth century women, on the other hand, had little career choice. The first thing that Gervase Markham mentions in *The English Housewife* is the need for a woman to be both modest and devout. 'Our English housewife must be of chaste thought, stout courage, patient, untired, watchful, diligent, witty,

Should the fire go out, it would be lit with a tinder box.

pleasant, constant in friendship. Full of good neighbourhood, wise in discourse, but not frequent therein, sharp and quick of speech, but not bitter or talkative, secret in her affairs, comfortable in her counsel, and generally skilful in all the worthy knowledges which do belong to her vocation.'[1] It was difficult enough for our female ancestors to reach such a pinnacle of perfection but in addition, many of the tasks that they were expected to master, in their role as a housewife, were both complex and

---

1 Best, Michael R. [ed.] Markham, Gervase. *The English Housewife,* 1986, McGill-Queen's University Press (1615), p. 8.

physically demanding. Undoubtedly, most women were also unpaid assistants to their husbands, in what ever vocation they followed. It was not just the mother of the family who was expected to run the household; she would normally be assisted by her children, particularly her daughters.

Fuel

A fire was essential for cooking, heating water, light, warmth and rubbish disposal. Ideally, the fire was kept alight continually. At night, night caps were used to keep the fire contained. Should the fire go out, it would be lit with a tinder box, by striking stone on flint and igniting material such as horse hair or linen, before transferring the blaze to the kindling. This gave rise to the expression 'strike a light'. Although the term electricity was first coined by William Gilbert in 1600, our Stuart ancestors had to rely on other fuels.[2] Fuels for the poor included furze,[3] bracken, broom and heather. There were regional variations, such as dried seaweed in coastal areas. Animal, particularly cow, dung was a popular fuel; it was very efficient and generated more heat than wood. The collecting of sufficient fuel to keep the fire going was a constant task, usually for the younger children. To supply a farm for the winter, some 1000 faggots were needed. Producing these would be twenty days' uninterrupted work for a skilled labourer but in practice, the faggots would probably be made in a more haphazard and slower, way by all members of the family who were physically capable. A faggot was made up from four armfuls of furze that would be gathered with one hand and cut with the other. The bundles were then bound with green branches and put into ricks.

In some areas, the cutting of wood was banned but it was acceptable to remove any dead wood that could be accessed 'by hook or by crook'; in other words with the use of the labourer's bill hook or the shepherd's crook. The need for sizeable timbers for shipbuilding meant that a regulation, of 1620, required twelve large trees per acre to be left for this purpose. Ideally, wood needed to dry for a year before being burnt.

It was only economical to transport coal by sea, so it was rarely used outside the immediate area. London's large concentration of population however meant that there was insufficient wood, so, by the seventeenth century, they were importing Newcastle coal. Coal was very dirty compared to other fuels and this did not help the urban environment. Town dwellers did not need to be quite so self sufficient as their rural counterparts. For them, bread and pies might be taken to the bakers for baking and the kettle only boiled when required, rather than being kept constantly on the fire; thus less fuel would be used.

Lighting

Most households' days began and ended with the daylight. The fire gave off a certain amount of additional light and all but the humblest of households would have supplemented this with some form of artificial lighting. The housewife was

---

2 See also Chapter 3 for a discussion of cooking methods and fuels.
3 Or gorse.

The Art and Mystery of Making WAX and TALLOW CANDLES.

The housewife was responsible for making candles for the family.

responsible for making the family's candles, to be used in a candle stick or lantern. Beeswax candles were expensive and thus for higher status households or special occasions. Tallow candles, with linen wicks, were made with animal fat, ideally from sheep or bullocks. These were cheaper but smelt less pleasant and gave off a dimmer light. The rush dip,[4] which might be held in a special holder, was for the poorest families. These again used animal fat but had wicks made from green rushes that had been softened in water, peeled and had the pith dried out, before being coated in the fat. All forms of candle had to be repeatedly dipped and cooled to increase the thickness. A fifteen inch rush dip, which would be about a quarter of an inch in diameter, burned for twenty to thirty minutes. The rush could be lit at both ends to give off extra light but this was an extravagance, as it burnt away twice as quickly. This practice is the origin of the expression 'burning the candle at both ends'. Oil lamps, in wealthy households, might use olive oil, imported from the Mediterranean. For the less well off, the cheaper but much smellier, option was animal or fish oil.

Water

Bathing had been more popular in Medieval times but went out of fashion in the sixteenth century, when it was believed that exposing the skin made it more likely to absorb miasmas, or bad smells and cause illness. Nonetheless, water was needed for washing, cleaning, laundry and cooking. Towns were dirtier, so, compared to rural areas, more washing and cleaning were required there. Nineteenth century social reformers suggested that, for health, each person needed at least two gallons of water a day and it is likely that our Stuart ancestors used similar amounts. This would have to be carried from the nearest well, spring, pump or river. With no drainage systems, dirty water also had to be disposed of. Although it may only have been thrown outside the cottage, it still involved some physical effort.

Transporting sufficient water for the family's needs was no easy task. Buckets might be made of canvas but were often wooden and thus extremely heavy, even when empty. Buckets could be carried in the hand, on the head, supported by a circlet of straw, or using a yoke. The average load was three gallons but an adult might carry up to six and a half.[5] There would also be a great deal of physical effort involved in pumping water or winding up buckets from wells. Some town wells, or those on large estates, had animal powered winches but this was not common. The water source might have been closer for urban dwellers but they may have had to queue to collect water, especially if there had not been much rain. Little wonder then, that our ancestors used water butts and hand dug ponds. By the seventeenth century, London had a piped water supply of sorts. Lead was prohibitively expensive so pipes were made of wood, which was prone to splitting; elm worked best. Some of London's water was piped in from Hertfordshire. In the 1690s, George Sorocold used a system of pumps and cisterns to supply other towns with piped water.

The development of country house gardens gave the aristocracy the incentive to

---

4   Rush dips became even more popular after the introduction of the candle tax in 1709.
5   A gallon of water weighs about 10lbs.

Transporting sufficient water for the family's needs was no easy task.

investigate ways of improving the water supply for their exotic plants. Hydrology became a flourishing science during the Restoration but this had little impact on the lives of most of the population.

Laundry

Wash day was traditionally on Monday. Clean clothes were normally put on on a Sunday, so this allowed the longest possible amount of time to get clothes dry. Another reason that housewives often stuck to the same day was because washing day might be a communal activity. It was easier to take clothes to the water source than vice versa, so women would often meet by the stream and wash together. Many town wells had washing blocks, for the pounding of the clothes, beside them. Less frequent wash days were a sign of social status as it implied that the family had sufficient supplies of clothing, bed and table linen to make weekly washing unnecessary.

The housewife would need to rise early to accomplish all that was required on wash day. More comfortably off households would have a copper in which to heat the water, the alternative was water heated over the fire or cold stream water. As with modern washing machines, agitation of the clothes was seen as necessary to remove dirt and in the seventeenth century, clothing was put on a washing stone and beaten with a laundry bat. This device, from which cricket bats probably derived, had many dialect names, including battledore and beetle. Alternatively, particularly in certain parts of the country, notably Scotland, clothes would be put in a tub and trampled on with bare feet.

The buck wash involved soaking the clothing in lye for several days, in a large bucket known as a bucking tub. This formed part of a great wash, rather than being a weekly activity. Buck was also a word used to describe fresh urine and this was often used in the process. Lye was a cleaning agent prepared by the women of the family. It was made using a special tub known as a lye dropper, a wooden vessel with holes in the bottom. Large stones would be placed in the tub followed by a layer of straw. This was covered with ash. Ash made from burning part-dried ferns in pots, to create potash,[6] worked best. Water was dripped on top and allowed to strain through for two or three days. The resulting mixture could be made into lye balls by adding water. A dozen of these ash balls, about three inches in diameter, would cost 2d. Soap could be made from animal fat;

Clothing was beaten with a laundry bat.

herbs would be added for a more palatable smell. Animal fat however had many other uses and it might be considered extravagant to use it for soap making. The other danger was prosecution, as there was both a monopoly[7] and substantial excise duty on soap production.[8]

To Take Stains of Fruit out of Linnen

Before you washeth it, rub every spot with a little butter, then set it scalding a while in hot milk, and when it is somewhat cool, rub the spotted places in the milk until the spots are quite out, then wash it in water and soap.

From Hannah Wolley's *Compleat Servant-maid*

---

6 This was potassium carbonate, rather than mined potash.
7 The Westminster Society of Soapmakers was given a 14 year monopoly in 1631. Soap manufacture was limited to within a mile of London or Bristol.
8 During the Commonwealth, the tax was 4/- a barrel.

2

COFFERS, CLYSTERS, COMFREY AND COIFS

Bleaching was accomplished using stale urine or animal dung. Urban areas often had a communal urine barrel for this and other purposes. Washing would also be laid out in the sun, on the bleaching ground, to help it to whiten. Other methods of stain removal involved the use of vinegar, fullers' earth, bran or white bread. The latter was particularly recommended for rubbing on delicate fabrics such as lace, in order to remove the stains. The art of starching came from the Low Countries in the sixteenth century. Starch was made from quickly boiled wheat but was probably not used by poorer households.

By the late seventeenth century, a form of mangle, involving a box full of stones resting on wooden rollers, had been devised but this was prohibitively expensive for all but the aristocracy. Wet clothing would be wrung out by hand, a

Wet washing was laid on a hedge to dry.

task that ideally required two people turning the garment in opposite directions. Wringing posts allowed clothing to be looped round and then twisted together by one person but this was less effective. Some Stuart housewives may have pegged items on a line, although the line might have been a horizontal, supported pole, rather than a rope. Otherwise, wet washing was laid on a hedge, or arranged in front of the fire to dry.

Ironing was not something that many ordinary housewives would have considered necessary. Those working as domestic servants for middle class households would have used sadirons,[9] heated by the fire, or box irons filled with hot coals or charcoal.

Cleaning

Despite it being difficult to achieve, a Stuart housewife would aspire to a clean home as cleanliness was a sign of moral rectitude; cleanliness was, quite literally, next to godliness. Floors would be swept regularly using a broom, or besom. These were made from birch twigs or heather. The bundle of twigs was usually about three foot long and ten to twelve inches in diameter. The twigs were bound to a sturdier handle of lime, hazel or birch using willow or hazel wands. Earth floors were covered with bracken or rushes to absorb cooking debris and mud and these were renewed regularly. Earth floors could also be damped down to lay the dust in dry weather. Goose wings made excellent feather dusters and chimneys were cleaned by pulling

9 Solid or flat irons.

holly branches through them. Bed bugs had arrived in this country in the sixteenth century, possibly as a result of the age of exploration. By 1682, they were causing serious concern[10] and the bug-destroying firm, Messers Tiffin and Son of London, was founded in 1695.

Horsetails or pewterwort were used for scrubbing pots and pans and cleaning pewter as they contain a natural non-stick. Fine sand and ground oyster shell were also used for cleaning pewter, brass and china and for scouring the bottom of cooking vessels. Silver might be washed with lye. It was also possible to wipe dishes with straw or clean them using bran. The bran stuck to the grease and could then be brushed off and fed to the pigs.

Feeding the Family

Many household tasks related to the production of food and drink. The Stuart housewife had to be proficient in jobs such as pickling, preserving, butter making, brewing and baking. Duties outside the house including milking the cows, feeding the chickens, collecting eggs, gardening and the care of bees. Bees needed to be caught when they swarmed in late spring and they would be housed in a straw hive or skep, which was usually placed on a stone

Floors wouild be swept regularly using a besom.

To Preserve Cherries

To every pound of cherries take a pound of sugar. That done, take a few cherries and strain them to make your syrup, and to every pound, a pound of sugar and cherries. Take a quarter of a pound of syrup, and this done, take your syrup and sugar and set it on the fire. Then put your cherries into your syrup and let them boil several times. After every boiling skim them with the backside of a spoon.

From Thomas Dawson's *The Good Housewife's Jewel*

---

10   Tryon, Thomas. *A Treatise of Cleanness in Meats and Drinks,* 1682, London, pp. 7-13.

niche against a wall. Although, by the 1600s, some families, primarily urban dwellers who were further up the social scale, were outsourcing some of these tasks, most rural women would need to be accomplished in all.

Brewing too might be done professionally but home brewing was still the norm. The malt, germinated barley required for beer making, was usually provided by a specialist maltster however Markham clearly expects the seventeenth century farmer's wife to be producing her own.[11] Hops would be added. These acted as a preservative, ensuring that the beer would keep. Ale, on the other hand, was made without hops and kept for only a week or so. Yeast was added to ensure fermentation. Yeast needed reasonably warm temperatures to begin fermentation. This could be accelerated by adding animal products to the mixture. Rabbit skins or slices of meat were often used for this purpose but a dead rat worked just as well. The first brew of the year was known as March beer. It was made in the spring using the fresh crop of malt and hops. It was best to leave this brew for twelve months before consumption and it would keep for several years.

Bees would be housed in a skep.

Straining Bees

Let no fire come near your honey, for fire softened the wax and dross, and makes them run with honey. Fire softeneth, weakeneth, and hindreth honey from purging. Break your combs small, when the dead empty combs are parted from the loaden combs into a sieve, born over a great bowl or vessel with two staves, and so let it run two or three days. The sooner you run it up, the better will it purge. Run your swarm honey by itself, and that shall be your best. The elder your hives are, the worse is your honey.

From William Lawson's *The Country Housewife's Garden*

11 Best, Michael R. [ed.] Markham, Gervase. *The English Housewife,* 1986, McGill-Queen's University Press, (1615), p. 180.

When to Pot Butter

Now although you may at any time betwixt May and September pot up butter, observing to do it in the coolest time of the morning. Yet the principal season of all is in the month of May only; for then the air is most temperate , and the butter will take salt the best, and the least subject to reesing.

From Gervase Markham's *The English Housewife*

Butter and cheese making were essential skills for most housewives. The majority of butter making was normally done in May and June, when the grass was greenest and the cows were giving the creamiest milk. Butter making was not a pleasant task. It was best achieved in a cold, damp dairy. The cream was skimmed off the milk and placed in a churn. It might take anything from twenty minutes to two hours of churning before the butter was produced. Churns might be of the plunge variety, where a wooden plunger was jerked up and down in a tall receptacle. Alternatively, there were the, more sophisticated, swing churns, which could make larger quantities. The butter was then washed and squeezed, to remove any excess liquid; the resulting buttermilk could be drunk or fed to the pigs. The butter was then heavily salted and stored in barrels, so that it would keep for the remainder of the year. Once made, the butter was primarily used for baking, rather than spreading. Markham suggested that churning should be done on Tuesdays and Fridays, ready for the markets that were customarily held on Wednesdays and Saturdays.[12] Butter for market, or for immediate use, would be patted into an oblong shape with small paddles or butter pats. A farmer's wife might have had her own wooden mould with which to stamp her butter with an identifying pattern.

Butter making was an essential skill.

---

12 Best, Michael R. [ed.], Markham, Gervase. *The English Housewife,* 1986 McGill - Queen's University Press, (1615), p. 171.

The Queen's Cheese

Take six quarts of the best stroakings, and let them stand till they are cold; then set two quarts of cream on the fire till 'tis ready to boil; then take it off, and boil a quart of fair water, and take the yolks of two eggs, and one spoonful of sugar, and two spoonfuls of runnet. Mingle all these together, and stir it till 'tis blood warm. When the cheese is come, use it as other cheese. Set it at night and the third day lay the leaves of nettles under and over it. It must be turned and wiped, and the nettles shifted every day, and in three weeks it will be fit to eat. This cheese is made between Michaelmas and Allhallowtide

From William Carew Hazlitt's *Old Cookery Books and Ancient Cuisine*

Cheese, or white meat, was eaten regularly and stored well. In order to make cheese, rennet was required. This came from the stomach of a young calf that had never eaten grass and calves would be slaughtered, when they were about two weeks old, especially for this purpose. Markham recommended laying in a good store of cheeselip bags, or rennet and when the bag was opened, the housewife was to 'pick out of [the curd] all manner of motes, chires of grass, or other filth gotten into the same.'[13] It was possible to use nettles or vinegar instead of rennet but these were not so effective.

The curds and whey would be separated and strained through muslin before being left to drain, in order to produce a soft cheese. To make hard cheese, in other words, one that would keep, a cheese press was needed, to squeeze out all the whey. The cheese had to be turned daily and a rind was created by wiping the outer surface with salt water. The cheese would be ready after two or three months and could be stored for a year.

Bread making was a daily task. Flour might be bought in ready milled but most housewives would produce small amounts for themsleves, using a hand mill. This was often preferable to taking corn for bulk grinding by the miller, for which there would be a charge. The expression 'a daily grind' refers to the hour or so each day that our Stuart ancestress would need to spend at her hand mill in order to produce sufficient flour for the family.

---

13 Best, Michael R. [ed.] Markham, Gervase. *The English Housewife,* 1986, McGill-Queen's University Press, (1615), p. 175.

Bear in mind that the seventeenth century housewife also needed to be cook, seamstress, gardener and nurse. For much of her married life she would be doing these tasks either whilst pregnant, or with a small baby in tow. It was hardly surprising that the daughters of the household were expected to assist their mothers from a very young age. In the 1600s, a woman's work truly was never done.

Further Reading

Best, Michael R. (ed.), Markham, Gervase. *The English Housewife,* 1986, McGill-Queen's University Press, (1615).

Bradley, R. M. *The English Housewife in the Seventeenth and Eighteenth Centuries,* 1912, Edward Arnold.

Clark, Alice. *Working Life of Women in the Seventeenth Century,* 1982, Routledge.

Davidson, Caroline. *A Woman's Work is Never Done: a history of housework in the British Isles 1650-1950,* 1986, Chatto and Windus.

Dawson, Thomas. *The Good Housewife's Jewel,* 1996, Southover Press, (1596/7).

Fraser Antonia. *The Weaker Vessel: woman's lot in seventeenth century England,* 2002, Orion Publishing Group.

Hole, Christina. *The English Housewife in the Seventeenth Century,* 1953, Chatto & Windus.

Mc Govern, Una. *Lost Crafts: rediscovering traditional skills,* 2008, Chambers.

Wolley, Hannah. *The Compleat Servant-maid: or, the young maiden's and family's daily companion,* Gale ECCO Print (9th edition 1719).[14]

<<**http://www.oldandinteresting.com/default.aspx**>> A history of domestic paraphernalia.

---

14   The first edition appeared in 1677.

CHAPTER 3

Cauldrons, Comfits, Coffins and Caudle: food and drink

Cooking Methods

Our ancestors' diet was governed by their cooking equipment and the availability of ingredients. By the late seventeenth century, all but the poorest homes had a hearth and a brick built chimney, even if they lacked an oven. The fuel that was used depended on what was obtainable locally and different fuels produced distinct types of heat, which in turn led to differing cooking methods. Peat, for example, gave off a gentle heat that was suitable for, amongst other things, clotted cream. Wood was the most popular fuel; a wood fire could be lit and a kettle boiled within twenty minutes. Coal was used but was believed, by some, to be bad for the health and an evil influence in a domestic setting.

Roasting was not an option for many families. It required a broach, or spit, a larger fireplace and the man, or child, power to turn the spit for several hours. Dogs provided a slightly less reliable form of power by being persuaded into a device resembling a large hamster wheel. Some richer Stuart households used clockwork jacks to turn the spit. As fat dripped from the joint it was collected in a dripping pan and used to baste the joint. The easiest way of cooking was boiling and this method was universal. It also required less fuel than roasting. Boiling was done in a large pot or cauldron over the open fire. Grain was added to water to make pottage,[1] a form of porridge to which vegetables, meat or fish could be added. The contents of the pottage varied with the season and the wealth of the family.

Keeping livestock over winter usually meant supplementing the animals' feed with items that might otherwise be eaten by people. Many animals therefore were slaughtered in the autumn, leaving only breeding stock for the following year. There was little fresh meat in winter, although meat that had been smoked or dried could be used. It was important to utilise as much of the beast as possible. Offal, or umbles, would be baked in a pastry case, giving us the phrase 'humble pie'. Problems of transportation and preservation meant that salt-water fish and shellfish were only available close to the sea. For those living inland, fish could be dried and fresh-water fish, including eels, were eaten. The wealthy might farm fish in their own fish ponds. Fish was particularly popular on fast days, such as Fridays and during Lent, when eating meat was forbidden.

---

1 Named for the cooking vessel.

The easiest way of cooking was boiling.

For most families, meat, albeit of an inferior quality, would be present in the majority of meals. Chicken was not a regular part of the diet, as the eggs were more valuable. If a family kept four chickens they should have been supplied with an egg a day, more during the summer months. The eggs were rarely eaten alone but were invaluable for baking. Turkeys were first imported into Britain in the fifteenth century and pigeons were often eaten. The union of the crowns, in 1603, heralded an increase in the consumption of Scottish beef. The rich and the proficient poachers amongst the poor, ate a variety of game: partridge, pheasant and venison, for example.

Many modern fruits and vegetables would not have been widely available 350 years ago and those that were had much shorter growing seasons. Swedes were not yet cultivated and tomatoes, initially known as love apples or golden apples, only reached Europe in the sixteenth century. Beet and root vegetables stored more easily than leafy vegetables, so turnips, carrots and parsnips could be used for most of the year. Until the end of the 1600s, British carrots were purple or white. There is some disagreement about exactly when the orange variety was brought from the Low Countries but the most popular theory is that they arrived with William of Orange, in whose honour the bright orange carrots had been favoured. Peas dried easily, making peas pottage a popular option. People were moving away from the Medieval

To Make A Lamb Pasty

Bone the lamb, and cut it four-square; lay beef suet at the bottom of your pasty, season the lamb with salt, pepper, minced thyme, nutmegs, cloves, and mace and lay it upon the suet, making a high border about it. Then turn over your sheet of paste, close it, and bake it. When it is baked, put in vinegar, the yolks of eggs, well beaten, and some sugar, or leave out the sugar if you please, and put in good gravy or the baking of the bones in claret.

From Hannah Wolley's *The Complete Servant-maid*

abhorrence of raw vegetables; salads were increasingly served. By the end of the century, John Evelyn devoted a whole book to salads and their dressings.[2]

Home grown fruits: apples, pears, plums and cherries, were generally available. Oranges and other imports were for the rich. Fruit such as bananas and pineapples were a novelty. The first banana to be brought to England, in the 1630s, was displayed in an apothecary's shop for a month as a curiosity. There was a reluctance to serve too much fruit, especially in its raw state. The loose stools that resulted, raised the fear of typhus and young children especially ate very little fruit for this reason. Dried fruit, such as raisins of the sun were used by those who could afford them. There were several arguments about the importation of currants, a monopoly held by the Levant Company[3] until 1629. In 1642, the importation of currants was forbidden because of the high levels of duty being paid on those that were being brought in from Venice. Although the ban only lasted for two years, few currents were brought in until the Restoration.

Puddings, previously baked in animal entrails, were, by the early seventeenth century, wrapped in a pudding cloth and lowered into the cooking pot for boiling. Sweet and savoury would be cooked together in this way. Meat, flavoured with herbs, could be placed in an earthenware pot, with a little butter. This was sealed with a pastry strip and submerged in the cauldron. The use of the sealed pot, or jug, reduced cooking time and was the principle behind the digester, a form of pressure cooker invented by the Frenchman Papin in 1682. Pies were baked in pastry casings or coffins. Initially, these coffins were a cooking method, intended to hold the ingredients together; the pastry would have been too hard to be eaten. Pottery pie ware was also

2 Evelyn, John. *Acetaria, a Discourse of Sallets,* 1996, Prospect Books (1699).
3 The Levant Company tried sub-contracting this monopoly in return for a levy of 5/6 per hundredweight.

used to make pies; even the top might be pottery. The hollow pottery handle, similar to a modern saucepan handle, provided a method of removing the hot pan from the fire safely. A stick would be inserted into the handle in order to lift it off the heat, so no oven gloves were required. Open pastry tarts were also popular and gradually it became customary to eat the pies' pastry casing as well as the contents.

Various novelty fillings were presented in pies, of both the pottery and pastry kind, in order to impress guests. This included live offerings: hence the 'four and twenty blackbirds'. The Duke and Duchess of Buckingham, entertaining Charles I in Rutland in the 1620s, served a child dwarf, Jeffery Hudson, in a cold pie.

Filling up the Family

Their lifestyle meant that our working Stuart ancestors needed roughly twice as many calories as modern man. Potatoes, still a delicacy, were considered to be a fruit. It was therefore thought that they should be served green, with unpleasant consequences for the consumer. In some circles, potatoes were believed to increase evil blood. In 1619, they were banned in Burgundy as a potential cause of leprosy however they did have their supporters; improved fertility being just one of the stated benefits. In 1664, John Forster wrote a pamphlet advocating the cultivation of the

potato. With the exception of low-lying areas of Britain, such as the fens, where a little wild rice was grown, rice was imported and thus beyond the means of the ordinary Stuart housewife. The wealthy used it for rice puddings rather than as part of a savoury course. The earliest reference to pasta (macaroni) in England was in a fourteenth century recipe book however it was not until the Georgian age of the grand tour that more frequent travel to Italy broadened its appeal. This left few options to stave off the hunger of families who were engaged primarily in manual labour, with appetites to match.

Subsisting largely on bread, cheese and peas, for the poor, food was bland and monotonous. Bread was normally baked daily, either in a bread oven, or by the side of the open fire. If a bread oven was used, the fire would be lit and when the stones were warm the fire would be raked out and the dough put inside. The oven door was then sealed with flour and water. Maintaining the oven at a constant temperature was virtually impossible. As the bread oven lost heat, pies, cakes and custards would be cooked. Finally, as it cooled further, it would be used for such tasks as drying cored and peeled apples. Once dried, the apples would be strung up like beads and hung from the ceiling.

White manchet bread was the preserve of the rich and considered to be better for health. This assumption was based on price, as white flour was more time consuming and thus more costly, to produce. Darker, ravelled bread or chete was for those further down the social scale and the darkest, rye based, carter's bread was for the poorest labourers. Oblys, small round loaves, were often produced. Servants would slice loaves horizontally. The top portion of the loaf was fed to the family, who became known as the 'upper crust', leaving the, slightly ashy, bottom part for the servants.

To Make Jumbles

To make the best jumbles, take the whites of three eggs and beat them well, and take off the veil; then take a little milk and a pound of fine wheat flour and sugar together finely sifted, and a few aniseeds as well rubbed and dried; and then work all together as stiff as you can work it, and so make them in what forms you please, and bake them in a soft oven upon white papers.

From Gervase Markham's *An English Housewife*

Recipe books, aimed at wealthy households, were produced regularly during the seventeenth century. The move towards increasing variety did begin to permeate down the social scale, particularly after the Restoration. Baking was no longer restricted to the heavy, rich cakes and biscuits of the Middle Ages. Jumbals, dough flavoured with caraway seeds or aniseeds, were wound into plaits or knots and baked. Sugar was increasingly imported after the Barbadian colonists began growing sugar cane on their plantations in the 1630s. Sugar was sold in loaves priced at 6d each, almost a day's wage for a labourer. The ostentatious use of such an expensive commodity as sugar was a sign of social status and wealthy households offered a variety of crystallised delicacies, comfits (sugar coated fruit or nuts) and confectionary, as a way of impressing their guests. The stems of the angelica plant, rosemary flowers and the roots of the elecampane were commonly served in this way. For ordinary families, honey provided a sweetener, together with items such as rosewater, sweet Cecily (chervil) roots or marigold (calendula) petals, which could be used fresh or dried. East India Company officers, returning on leave, brought with them a taste for spices that only those of higher status could afford. The ordinary housewife depended instead upon the herbs from her garden to add interest to the family's diet.

The rich ate their main meal of the day around 4.00pm. Under the Tudors, Sumptuary Laws had restricted the number of removes, or courses, which could be served during a banquet; the quantity of dishes varying with social status. For our ordinary ancestors things were very different. The working man ate at dusk, when his day's labours were over. There was little finesse about his dining: wooden dishes, a knife that was probably also used for household tasks and spoons made of wood or horn where fingers wouldn't do.

Storing and Preserving
Keeping food fit for consumption was a problem. The very wealthy had ice houses. These were underground chambers built in the garden and enabled ice cream to be produced and food to be kept cool. The ice was covered in straw to preserve it

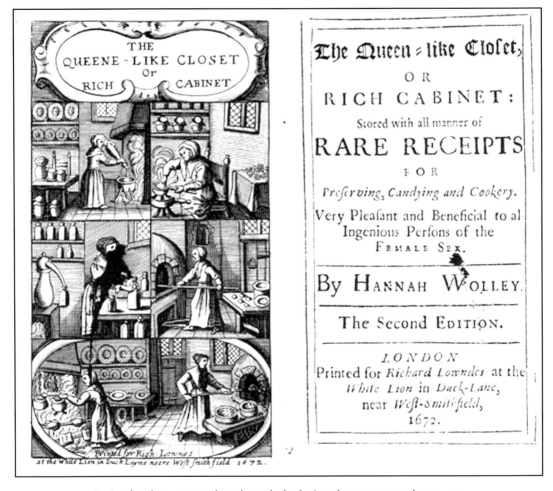

Recipe books were produced regularly during the seventeenth century.

however the process was very inefficient, especially in the summer, so refrigeration was not a practical option. Stone larders or slate and marble slabs did help to keep things, such as dairy produce, at low temperatures but not for extended periods. The lengthy sea voyages of the sixteenth century made the long-term preservation of food essential and new methods were devised. Pickling, of crops such as beetroot and potting were common. Dried peas were a staple of the seventeenth century diet. It was possible to preserve hot food by swimming over a layer of fat, ideally clarified mutton fat. As this cooled it created a seal but this would break if the bowl was moved.

The most efficient way of preserving meat or fish was to smoke it. The annual pig killing would be followed by the smoking of large hams. Some chimneys incorporated smoke holes for this purpose. The family pig was vital to sustaining the household and would provide food for up to six months. Every part of the animal was used, the offal being eaten first as it could not be preserved. Seventeenth century recipe books reflect this dependence on parts of the animal that are now rarely consumed. Markham describes the way in which a cow's udder should be prepared. Cloves

To Make Fritters of Sheep's Feet

Take your sheep's feet, slit them and set them a stewing in a silver dish with a little strong broth and salt, with a stick of cinnamon, two or three cloves, and a piece of an orange pill. When they are stewed, take them from the liquor and lay them upon a pye-plate cooling. When they are cold, have some good fritter-batter made with sack, and dip them therein. Then have ready to fry them, some excellent clarified butter very hot in a pan, and fry them therein. When they are fryed wring in the juyce of three or four oranges, and toss them once or twice in a dish, and so serve them to the table.

From W. M's The Compleat Cook

would be added before it was boiled, then it was roasted and served with bread-crumbs, sugar and cinnamon.[4] Mary Kettilby's collection of receipts, or recipes, gives instructions on how a calf's head could be roasted. 'After the head is nicely washed and pick'd, take out the brains and tongue; make a large quantity of forc'd-meat, with veal and suet well season'd, fill the hole of the head; skewer it, and tie it together upon the spit; one hour and an half roasts it. Beat up the brains with a little sage and parsley finely shred, a little salt, and the yolks of two or three eggs; boil and blanch the tongue, cut it in large dice, and fry that and the brains, as also some of the forc'd meat in balls, and some slices of bacon. The sauce is strong broth, with oysters, mushrooms, capers and a little white wine thicken'd.'[5]

Beverages

Apart from those who had easy access to a spring or uncontaminated well, in the 1600s, the drinking of water was not recommended. Milk was readily available, even in towns, but without pasteurisation, drinking milk straight from the cow brought its own problems. In any event, the real value of milk was for the making of cheese and butter and to drink it was regarded as wasteful.

Coffee and chocolate were beverages of the rich and were usually drunk in coffee or chocolate houses in large towns as part of a social ritual, rather than to quench thirst. Coffee is believed to have arrived in England in 1650. A Jew named Jacobs may

---

4 Best, Michael R. (ed.) Markham, Gervase. *The English Housewife,* 1986, McGill-Queens University Press, (1615), p. 89.
5 Kettilby, Mary et. al. *A Collection of above Three Hundred Receipts in Cookery, Physick and Surgery; for the use of all Good Wives, Tender Mothers and Careful Nurses',* 2010, Nabu Press (5th edition 1734), p. 24.

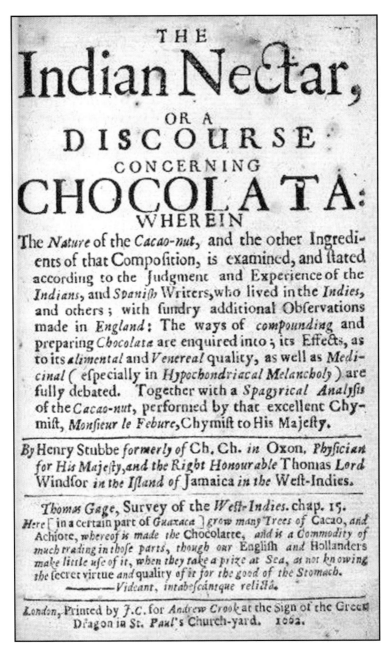

THE

Indian Nectar,

OR A

DISCOURSE

CONCERNING

CHOCOLATA:

WHEREIN

The *Nature* of the *Cacao-nut*, and the other Ingredients of that Compofition, is examined, and ftated
according to the Judgment and Experience of the
Indians, and *Spanifh* Writers, who lived in the *Indies*,
and others; with fundry additional Obfervations
made in *England*: The ways of *compounding* and
preparing *Chocolata* are enquired into; its Effects, as
to its *alimental* and *Venereal* quality, as well as *Medicinal* (efpecially in *Hypochondriacal Melancholy*) are
fully debated. Together with a *Spagyrical Analyfis*
of the *Cacao-nut*, performed by that excellent Chymift, *Monfieur le Febure*, Chymift to His Majefty.

By Henry Stubbe *formerly of* Ch. Ch. *in* Oxon, *Phyfician
for His Majefty, and the Right Honourable* Thomas Lord
Windfor *in the Ifland of* Jamaica *in the* Weft-Indies.

Thomas Gage, Survey of the *Weft-Indies*. chap. 15.
Here [in a certain part of *Guaxaca*] *grow many Trees of* Cacao, *and*
Achiote, *whereof is made the* Chocolatte, *and is a Commodity of
much trading in thofe parts, though our* Englifh *and* Hollanders
*make little ufe of it, when they take a prize at Sea, as not knowing
the fecret virtue and quality of it for the good of the Stomach.*
———*Videant, intabefcántque relictá.*

London, Printed by *J.C.* for *Andrew Crook* at the Sign of the Green
Dragon in St. *Paul's* Church-yard. 1662.

Coffee and chocolate were beverages of the rich.

have been the first to open a coffee house, in Cornhill, London but there are also claims that the Queen's Lane coffee house in Oxford, which opened in 1654, was the first. Chocolate quickly followed, in 1657. Despite tea (tcha) being renowned as the national drink of the English, it was not until the time of Charles II that the habit of drinking China tea was popularised. Herbal teas had long been used by all classes but these were largely consumed for medicinal purposes rather than for refreshment. In a similar way, caudle, ale or wine heated and thickened with egg yolk, was regarded as a restorative to which sugar, honey, ginger or cinnamon could be added. Metheglin was essentially an herbal tea, commonly lemon balm or rosemary, which had been mixed with honey. The foreign influences heralded by the Restoration, in 1660, provided many more options for metheglin recipes. Non-carbonated soft drinks, made from lemon juice, honey and water, were known in seventeenth century. The Compagnie de Limonadiers was granted the Parisian lemonade monopoly in 1676. Endeavours were also made to replicate the effervescent spa spring waters, resulting in carbonated beverages.

Drink for the common man was normally small beer, the brewing process removing the impurities from the water, although it was to be another 200 years before the role of bacteria was understood. The other advantage that beer had over water was that its calorific content gave it a nutritional value. Later, nineteenth century temperance movements were thought to lead to malnutrition for the poor who signed the pledge. Beer was produced by professional brewers and also in the home. The brewers' initial brew produced beer at 8% proof, similar to modern wines. This was re-brewed with additional water to leave a product that resembled present day beer and finally brewed again resulting in a small beer, from which almost all alcoholic content had been removed. Gervase Markham provided recipes for a variety of ales and beers.[6] Beer contained both malt and hops but for ale, the hops were optional. The addition of fermented honey and spices to ale produced drinks such as hydromel, bragget and mead. From the 1630s, beer could be sold in bottles but wine continued to be sold by the cask as the retailing of wine in bottles was prohibited in 1638.

To Make Strong Mead

To four gallons of water, put eighteen pounds of honey; beat the whites of four eggs, stir them in with the honey till it all be melted; scum it well as long as it boils, and be sure it boil an hour and a half. If you like the taste, you may put a sprig of Rosemary in the boiling. When it is cold, work it with a toast, spread with yeast; and when you put it in the vessel, hang therein one nutmeg, the weight of that in mace, and the same quantity in cloves, with four races of ginger, in a piece of muslin; the spice must be beaten; put in the peel of two lemons. When it has done working, stop it up, and let it stand six months, before you bottle it.

From Mary Kettilby's *A Collection of above Three Hundred Receipts in Cookery*

---

6 Best, Michael R. (ed.) Markham, Gervase. *The English Housewife,* 1986, McGill-Queens University Press, (1615), pp. 204-211.

Wines, such as malmsey and sack, were imported, mainly from France, Spain and Italy; brandy was another French import. Aqua Vitae was a generic name given to distilled wine although spirits were not commonly drunk. In 1689, in an effort to encourage home distilleries and in response to deteriorating relations with France, the importation of spirits was banned. Usquebath was an early form of whisky, one of the constituents of usquebath recommended by W M in his 'A Queen's Delight'[7] was ambergreece, a wax-like and extremely expensive, substance vomited by the sperm whale. There were also alcoholic drinks that verged on being foods and were often recommended for invalids. Hypocras was a spiced wine that was served hot. Syllabub, which was not popular until the later seventeenth century, involved adding sugar, cream and spices to cider, whereas a posset consisted of ale, bread, milk and spices.

Apart from home made fruit wines,[8] wine and spirits were increasingly out of reach of the labouring population, particularly after an excise tax was imposed in 1643. This was meant to be a war time measure but it was not repealed and alcoholic drink continued to attract tax. Cider drinking was more affordable but was only popular in apple growing areas such as Kent, Hereford, Gloucestershire, Worcestershire and the West Country. Perry, the pear equivalent, was largely confined to the Welsh Marches.

Inns and Alehouses

It was possible for our Stuart ancestors to drink alcohol outside the home. In general, inns provided food, drink and accommodation. The tavern, or ordinary, served food but did not provide for overnight guests and the alehouse, or tippling-house, was for

7   M., W. *The A Queen's Delight*, 1984, Prospect Books, (1671), p. 23.
8   Elderberry, cherry and gillyflower were common.

the consumption of drink only. Confusingly, the distinctions are blurred and 'alehouse' became a generic term that was used for anywhere where alcoholic drink could be purchased. These drinking establishments were not intended to attract local, social drinkers. Their purpose was to provide for travellers and to sell small beer, for home consumption, to those who lacked the equipment to brew their own.

The first Stuart laws to control alcohol consumption were passed during the reign of James I. These included the 1604 statute *'To Restrain the Inordinate Haunting and Tippling of Inns, Alehouses, and other Victualling Houses'*. This allowed the working man to remain in the alehouse for no more than one hour, whilst he ate his lunch. Any locals found on the premises for longer, on a working day, would be fined three farthings, or put in the stocks for four hours; the innkeeper would incur a ten shilling fine. Some landlords attempted to circumvent this regulation by owning two drinking establishments in close proximity and encouraging customers to move from one to the other when their hour was up. Drinking on a Sunday was restricted to travellers. Justices of the Peace were responsible for upholding licensing laws and their duties in this respect are comprehensively described in Dalton's *'The Countrey Justice'*.[9] In 1627, an *'Act for the Better Suppressing of Unlicensed Alehouse Keepers'* meant that the selling of alcohol without a license attracted a twenty shilling fine. Defaulters would be publicly whipped; a second offence resulted in one month in the house of correction. An established inn was only bound by these laws if they wanted to serve locals, those who lived within two miles of the premises. Closing time was 9.00pm in

9 Dalton, Michael. *The Countrey Justice: conteyning the practise of the justices of the peace,* 2004, The Lawbook Exchange Ltd., (1655), pp. 24-27.

winter and 10.00pm in summer. Statutes also regulated the price of drink. A quart of best ale or beer, or two quarts of small beer, was one penny; the fine for charging anything in excess of this was twenty shillings.

These regulations were a response to the perceived problems caused by drunkenness and riotous behaviour and owed something to the Puritanical outlook of James I. In 1606, an *'Act for Repressing the Odious and Loathsome Sin of Drunkenness'* was passed and the first offence of drunkenness attracted a five shilling fine or six hours in the stocks. Games such as cards, dice and bowls were also forbidden, both on the premises and in the inn yard. Later in the century, the consumption of, newly arrived, coffee, tea and chocolate was equally frowned upon and in 1676, a petition was presented calling for a ban on these drinks as well as brandy. It was not so much the drinks themselves but the social ambience that accompanied public drinking that led to the objections.

For the Stuart housewife, providing three meals a day for the family required ingenuity and sheer hard physical effort. Her supply of ingredients and cooking methods were at best unreliable and labour saving devices a thing of the future.

Further Reading

Several of the C17th recipe books are available as Internet downloads.

Best, Michael R. (ed.) Markham, Gervase. *The English Housewife,* 1986, McGill-Queens University Press, (1615).

Brears, Peter. *Food and Cooking in 17th Century Britain,* 1985, English Heritage.

Dalton, Michael. *The Countrey Justice: conteyning the practise of the justices of the peace,* 2004, The Lawbook Exchange Ltd., (1655),

Dawson, Thomas. *The Good Housewife's Jewel,* 1996, Southover Press, (1596/7).
Digby, Sir Kenelm. *The Closet of Sir Kenelm Digby Opened,* 2007, Echo Library, (1669).
Evelyn, John. *Acetaria, a Discourse of Sallets,* 1996, Prospect Books, (1699).
French, Richard Valpy. *Nineteen Centuries of Drink in England: A History,* 1884, Longmans Green.
Hartley, Dorothy. *Food in England,* 1954, Piatkus.
Hazlitt, William Carew. *Old Cookery Books and Ancient Cuisine,* 2006, Bibliobazaar, (1902).
Kettilby, Mary et. al. *A Collection of above Three Hundred Receipts in Cookery, Physick and Surgery; for the use of all Good Wives, Tender Mothers and Careful Nurses',* 2010 Nabu Press, (5th edition 1734).[10]
M., W. *The Compleat Cook* and *A Queen's Delight,* 1984, Prospect Books, (1655 & 1671).
Murrell, John. *A New Book of Cookerie,* 1972, Da Capo Press, (1615).
Peachey, Stuart. *The Tipplers Guide to Drink and Drinking in the early C17th,* 1992, Stuart Press.
Tannahill, Reay. *Food in History,* 1988, Penguin.
Wolley, Hannah. *The Compleat Servant-maid: or, the young maiden's and family's daily companion,* 2010, Gale ECCO Print, (9th edition 1719).[11]
Wolley, Hannah. *The Queen-like Closet or Rich Cabinet,* 2007, The Essential Book Market, (1672).
<<**www.foodtimeline.org**>> A timeline of when various foods were introduced, with links to additional information.
<<**www.godecookery.com/engrec/engrec.html**>> C17th English Recipes.

---

10   The first edition appeared in 1714.
11   The first edition appeared in 1677.

CHAPTER 4

Bucket-tops, Bodices, Bum Rolls and Britches: clothing

As with other aspects of seventeenth century life, sources giving details of the clothing of the working classes are rare. Like other features of Stuart times, fashions permeated down the social scale, with simplified and cheaper options of middle class clothing being worn by their poorer counterparts. There may have been some slight regional differences but clothing for our ordinary ancestors remained basically the same throughout the 1600s. The Puritan influence, advocating plainer styles, was particularly noticeable prior to and during the Commonwealth.

Underclothing
There were no close fitting undergarments. Female underwear was the shift; a nightdress-like garment, normally made from linen, with drawstrings at the neck and wrists. The men would wear a shirt, a shorter garment with a collar. Shifts and shirts were put on clean on a Sunday, in order to attend church and would be left on for a week. Thus the shift or shirt was night wear and by day, additional clothing was put on top. Those who aspired to white linen attempted to bleach the clothing in a bucket of stored urine but practicality meant that these garments were often off white. Most working class people could have afforded at least two shirts or shifts, so one could be worn whilst the other was being washed or, more particularly, dried; not an easy task in the British climate. Although modern usage has changed the meaning slightly, it is believed that the term shiftless, in the seventeenth century sense of being without resources, may come from the women who were too poor to own a second shift. Whilst their one garment was being dried they would find it difficult to get work as they would be improperly dressed. They thus became 'shiftless women'.

Women's Clothing
Over the centuries, conceptions of feminine modesty and beauty have changed. For Stuart women, the elbows and ankles had to be covered. This was considered more important than covering the breast. It was desirable for a woman to bear a large number of children in order to ensure that sufficient survived to contribute to the family economy and support their parents in old age. If a wife could do this without dying in the process it was an advantage and saved the man the trouble of finding a replacement. Consciously or sub-consciously therefore men were attracted by child bearing hips. Then, as now, women cheated in order to appear attractive. A bum-roll was worn to enhance the hips. This was a sausage shaped, linen item, stuffed with

horse hair or straw and tied round the waist. It was covered by a heavy petticoat. The petticoat was made of pure wool, as was a coat but it was smaller than a coat, hence petite, from the French. It was not until Victorian times that petticoat came to mean an undergarment. The petticoat was an expensive item, not in monetary terms but because of the time that was invested by the housewife in its production. For this reason, most women had only one petticoat and it had to last many years. It might have multiple fastenings at the front, either buttons, of wood or horn, or ties, so that it could be let out during pregnancy. An apron was essential; partly to cover any gap in the front but also to help keep the petticoat clean as it would not have been washed.

The laced bodice normally had elbow length sleeves, although a sleeveless bodice might be worn during the summer. The bodice was tight fitting at the waist with square panels extending over the hips. Front lacing was the most common; dressing in a back-laced bodice required the assistance of a servant, so was reserved for the wealthy. Most women laced their bodices loosely, in a criss-cross fashion. As with modern shoelaces, bodices could also be laced so they resembled a ladder. This style was adopted by the Puritans, who believed that the tighter lacing thus achieved helped to discipline the body and that a loose (laced) woman was immoral. Their preferred style of bodice lacing meant that the Puritans became known as 'straight-laced' women; the term later being applied to those whose personality resembled that of the Puritans. In the seventeenth century, corsets were stuffed with wood, so would have been very restrictive for the working classes and were therefore rarely worn by most women. Stays would also be wooden and these might be carved and given as a love gift, as they were worn close to the heart.

Female attire was completed with a linen collar worn round the neck and a coif to cover the hair. Although a single woman might wear her hair long and loose, one of the only assets by which she might capture a husband, a married woman would cover her hair as a sign of her status. Removing the coif so as to appear single, perhaps in order to enjoy the company of young men, was referred to as 'letting your hair down'. Woollen shawls or capes would provide warmth.

Men's Clothing

Men might wear a long sleeved coat in colder weather but normally a sleeveless woollen doublet or jerkin was worn over the shirt. The heavily padded garments of the sixteenth century were no longer fashionable. An alternative was the leather jerkin, or buff coat. Knee length woollen britches, or breeches, would be worn over hose, thin knitted stockings. Bearing in mind that, for most of the year, our seventeenth century ancestors were walking on damp grass or mud, women, with their floor length petticoats, would frequently have wet woollen cloth round their ankles. Men with their hose, that could be easily washed or dried, or boots, did not have to suffer in the same way. Headgear might be a Monmouth cap, which was a knitted skull cap, or a high-crowned felt hat with a deep brim, known as a capotain. These hats became less tall as the century progressed and by the late 1600s, the three-cornered hat had made an appearance. Woollen hats in the form of a balaclava were also worn.

Footwear

Footwear was for bad weather or the better-off. Both men and women might wear leather shoes, called latchets. These had either a flat leather sole or hobnails and could be quite slippery. For men who could afford it, bucket-top boots, that could be pulled up over the knee for protection, might be worn. Frequent riding wore out the soft top of the boot, so an additional piece of, butterfly-shaped, leather might be strapped over the uppers of each boot for protection. A working man could have shorter boots that laced up the front, known as start-ups. Both latchets and boots came as identical pairs, with no differentiation between the left and right foot. Clogs were worn but these were not like the solid wood Dutch clogs. Shaped wooden soles, made from alder, birch, beech or willow, would be attached to a leather upper. Wealthy women might aspire to silk slippers, probably French imports. To protect these she could wear overshoes or pattens. In the seventeenth century, the wooden soles were usually raised off the mud with an iron ring. Heavy and totally inflexible, these were

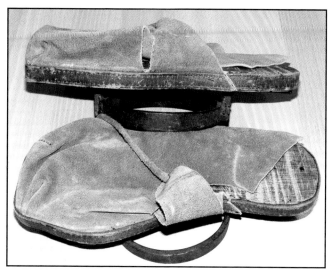
A woman would wear pattens to protect her silk slippers.

very difficult to walk in but achieved the aim of preserving the expensive silk footwear.

Rich and Poor, Old and Young

Styles of clothing were similar for all classes but the quality indicated the status of the wearer. Silk shirts, lace and silver buttons were all for the well off, as was deep black clothing; a lasting black dye being very difficult and expensive to achieve. The fact that seventeenth century wills often mention clothing, including items such as 'my third best suit of clothes to my son ….', indicates the value of such things, even to families that were of sufficient status to leave a will. Children's clothing was a miniature version of their parents'. Young boys, up to the age of about seven, were dressed in what we would consider to be female clothing, although, at the time, it was just seen as clothing for children. Anecdotally this has been associated with protection from witchcraft. Witches were thought to be intelligent enough to want to harm the most important children, in other words the boys. By dressing boys and girls in an identical fashion, the witches would be confused and the boys would be safe. In fact, the shift and petticoat were less quickly outgrown than traditional masculine styles of dress and it was also more practical for a child who was not toilet trained. In the seventeenth century, seven was considered to be the age of reason and for working class boys, might be the stage at which they began to earn a living and thus they would need to be more appropriately attired.

Spinning and Weaving

Now we turn our attention to how the clothing was made. Most, if not all, of the process was done at home, although it was possible to use professional spinners, weavers or dyers or to buy ready-made cloth, if the family's finances allowed. Even if the work was outsourced, the good housewife was expected to understand the process in order that she was not sold an inferior product. Gervase Markham states

that, 'our English housewife, after her knowledge of preserving and feeding her family, must learn also how, out of her own endeavours, she ought to clothe them outwardly and inwardly, outwardly for defence from the cold and comeliness to the person; and inwardly, for cleanliness and neatness of the skin, whereby it may be kept from the filth of sweat, or vermin; the first consisting of woollen cloth, the latter of linen.'[1]

There were many stages involved in the production of woollen clothing, beginning with shearing the sheep. The length and colour of the fleece depended on the type of sheep and some were more suitable for certain fabrics than others. The breed of sheep

Fleeces would be laid on racks in hot sunshine.

1   Best, Michael R. (ed.) Markham, Gervase. *The English Housewife*, 1986, McGill-Queens University Press, (1615), p. 146.

available to our ancestors depended very much upon where they lived and it would be likely to have been used for both meat and wool. If the family owned a sheep, it might not require any financial outlay to produce a woollen garment but it was very costly in terms of the time that was required and for this reason, clothing was a valued possession. Firstly, the fleeces needed to be washed. This was normally done in a copper, if the family were wealthy enough to have one, or over the fire. The plant soapwort was often added to the water to aid the cleansing process; alternatively the roots of the red campion could be used. Not only is a wet fleece incredibly heavy and difficult to handle but the Stuart housewife had the problem of getting it dry. Fleeces would be laid on racks in hot sunshine and turned regularly. It might take four days of good weather for a thick fleece to dry. Once

The fleece would be carded using a teasel.

dried, the fleece would be combed or carded, using a teasel, to remove any pieces of twig or leaf and to get the fibres lying in one direction ready for spinning. The medium length fleeces would be combed in order to produce better quality worsteds or jersey. Carding was more suitable for short wool or for wool that was going to be fulled or napped. Carding involved less effort than combing and was more likely to be the option for the ordinary housewife.

According to Thomas Caesar, writing in 1596,[2] there were three types of spinning. A great wheel, the traditional 'Sleeping Beauty' wheel, could be used to produce a woollen yarn. A smaller wheel would result in garnsey or jersey yarn, so called because it was associated with the Channel Islands. Finally spinning could be accomplished 'upon the rock', using a drop spindle, a method known since ancient times. This option was accessible to all as it involved no expensive equipment and it could be worked on the move, whilst the busy housewife was supervising children or other household activities. This form of spinning produced a worsted yarn.

Many households would own their own basic loom and the spun wool would be strung across to form the warp thread. The weft was then woven through it in various ways. Most home weaving would be plain weave, with the weft thread going

2 Quoted in Kerridge, Eric. *Textile Manufacturers in Early Modern England,* 1986, Manchester University Press, p. 159.

over and then under the alternate warp threads. Twill was produced by putting the weft over one warp thread and then under the next two, thus creating diagonal ridges in the cloth.

Fulling, was a method of matting the cloth. This was usually accomplished in a fulling mill, where the cloth would be beaten with large hammers. Fulling could be done at home, where beating might be done with hands or feet. Felting was also the result of thickening the cloth by beating. Napping raised the fibres of woven cloth and could be carried out using a teasel. Fulled cloth might be put on tenterhooks, stretched on a frame and suspended in an outdoor area known as a tenterground, to ensure that it dried flat and held its shape.

Wool could be knitted instead of woven. Knitting developed from nal-binding, a form of one-needled knitting, which produced a stretchy fabric and

A drop spindle was an option accessible to all.

was probably Scandinavian in origin. Hose could be knitted using jersey wool. William Lee's knitting machine had been invented in the late sixteenth century but Elizabeth I refused to grant it a patent. By the 1600s, machines began to be used to produce woollen and later silk, stockings. Lucetting was a method of producing woollen cords that could be used as fastenings. The lucette was a two pronged wooden implement that worked on the same principle as French knitting.

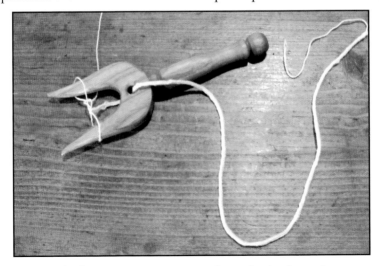

The lucette was a two pronged wooden implement.

Dyeing

An analysis of wills of the time[3] suggests that 75% of clothing was un-dyed and this percentage would have been likely to be higher amongst those who were not wealthy enough to leave a will. Hopkins and Peachey also found that town dwellers were more likely to sport bright colours than their rural counterparts. The natural colours of the wool did result in a range of, mostly fairly muted, hues but for those wishing to be more colourful, dyeing was necessary. It is possibly to dye in the wool, in other words before weaving but it was more common to weave first. It was necessary to remove the grease from the wool, in a process known as scouring, so that the dye could take. This was done by soaking in sig (stale urine[4]) or by using fuller's earth, a soft clay-like substance.

Dyeing could be substantive, which meant no additives apart from the natural dye were required; indigo fell into this category. More common was adjective dyeing, where a mordant, normally a metal salt, was employed as a fixative. Iron, copper or alum might be used in this way. The age of exploration meant that, by the seventeenth century, new dyes were available from many parts of the world. In 1630, a Dutch chemist called Drebbel used cochineal and tin to produce a bright red dye. This became available at the famous dye works in Bow, London. These exotic dyes came at a price that was beyond many of our ancestors.

Dyeing in the wood involved the use of logwood, which came from Central America and was introduced into England in 1614. Logwood[5] was not only the name of the tree but also of the dye that was produced from its heartwood. The bark and sapwood were removed and shavings were produced from the heartwood. These were aged or fermented before being used as a dye. At various times, the importation of logwood was prohibited or subject to a monopoly. In 1688, James II attempted to encourage the dyeing industry by banning the export of un-dyed cloth.

Contemporary recipe books, such as Gervase Markham's 'The English Housewife', first published in 1615,[6] give details of how certain colours could be achieved. Native

---

To Dye Wool Blue

To dye wool blue; take a good store of old chamber lye, and set it on the fire; then take half a pound of blue anil, byse, or indigo and beat it small in a mortar; and then put it into the lye; and when it seethes put in your wool.

From Gervase Markham's *The English Housewife*

---

3 Peachey, Stuart and Hopkins, David. *Dyeing Clothes of the Common People 1580-1660*, 2001, Stuart Press, p. 11.
4 There were various dialect words for stale urine, including 'lant' in Lancashire.
5 Also known as Blockwood.
6 Best, Michael R. (ed.) Markham, Gervase. *The English Housewife*, 1986, McGill-Queens University Press, (1615).

grown woad was used to create blue, although French woad was more successful. Imported indigo was better still and the upper classes often chose blue as the colour for their servants' livery. It was also popular as a school uniform, hence the Bluecoats' schools in many towns. Some areas, including Coventry, Exeter, Taunton and Tiverton were particularly noted for producing blue dyes. Madder roots gave a red colour, these were available at home but many were also imported from the Low Countries. Blackberry or elderberry were a cheaper alternative but did not produce a very fast dye. References to yellow clothing, usually made using the weld plant, are rarer in contemporary documents and there is a suggestion that the wearing of yellow hose was associated with lax morals. Green was a colour favoured by the higher classes and whilst professional dyers might re-dye a blue cloth with yellow to produce green, it could also be achieved by using comfrey or sage, together with a mordant. Black was difficult to obtain, particularly one that didn't fade quickly. Oak apples would be used on a cloth that was already dyed dark red or dark blue. Although deep black

was normally for the rich, more faded versions were worn by all classes. All colours could be brightened by the addition of fresh urine, known as buck.

Dyeing was a very smelly process, with some colours resulting in more noxious odours than others. Copper vessels were used by professional dyers but home dyeing would probably be done in a wooden barrel; iron cauldrons compromised the dyeing process.

Making Linen

Shirts, shifts and aprons were commonly made from linen. Fortunately, flax, from which it is made, grows well in the Northern European climate. By the seventeenth century, linen was less likely to be fully home-produced than in earlier eras. Flax was harvested in July and this was done by pulling up the whole plant, rather than it being cut, as corn would be. The flax or hemp plants had to be retted, soaked to reveal the fibres. Dew, or field, retting required leaving the plant on damp grass for six weeks and turning it regularly to produce a silvery-grey fibre. It was also possible to create a golden or creamy fibre by retting in water. This was achieved either by pond retting, submerging the flax in stagnant water for a few days, or, for better quality, stream retting under moving water for two or three weeks. Retted fibres were then scutched using a flat-bladed wooden flail known as a swingle. This broke down the plant to remove the woody stems. Finally the flax was hackled, or combed, before spinning. The wheels that were used differed from those that spun wool. Flyer spinning wheels or flax wheels were needed and a treadle wheel was developed in the early seventeenth century. This had the advantage that both the spinner's hands were free for guiding the fibres. Flax could also be spun using a drop spindle, with a distaff to hold the prepared fibres. By the end of the Stuart period, a two-handed flax wheel had been developed. Flax spinning could be done by children as young as six or seven and wheels were often provided in charity schools, especially in key linen producing areas. Flax fibres needed to be wetted for spinning, either by putting them in the mouth or wetting with a licked thumb. The weaving of the spun flax might also have been done in the home or could have been completed by a professional weaver.

The Watering of Hemp or Flax

The best water is the running stream, and the worst is the standing pit. Yet because hemp is a poisonous thing, and infecteth the water, and destroyed all kind of fish, it is more fit to employ such pits and ditches as are least subject to annoyance, except you live near some great broad and swift stream, and then in the shallow parts thereof you may water without danger.

From Gervase Markham's *The English Housewife*

Linen was much more difficult to dye than wool so was normally left in its natural colour. The better off wore the finest linen made from long, or line, fibres, whilst poorer people wore a coarser linen made from hemp or the shorter fibres, known as tow. For those who aspired to white linen, bleaching would be needed. This was a three stage process. First the cloth would be subjected to bucking, boiling in an alkali solution or lye; wood ash, soap, stale urine or kelp might be used for this. Then the cloth would be laid out in the sun for up to a fortnight for grassing, or crafting. At this stage the linen needed to be kept damp to allow the lye to take effect, without damaging the cloth. Finally the cloth was soured with bran or stale milk to neutralise the lye. For good quality linen, beetling, pounding the cloth to produce a shiny fabric with closed fibres, was needed.

Other Materials
Cotton garments, referred to in early seventeenth century documents such as wills or inventories, may not have been made of cotton in the modern sense, unless the family was very wealthy. These were probably items made from a woollen fabric that was produced by cottoning, or friezing, the cloth to raise the nap. This was usually done using poorer quality fleeces. In 1620, restrictions were relaxed and it became legal to

use what were known as new draperies. These were lighter materials, brought to England by Huguenot immigrants and included taffetas, bays and silks. James I wanted to stimulate an English silk industry and in 1608, he issued an edict encouraging the Lord Lieutenants to plant thousands of mulberry trees to this end. Cambridge University is known to have paid 18/- for 300 plants at this time. Unfortunately James introduced the black mulberry and silk worms need the white variety so his plan failed.

The East India Company began to import Indian calico in the 1630s but like other imports, these were expensive. The seventeenth century also saw the production of fustian, a fabric with a linen warp but a cotton weft thread. By the mid-seventeenth century, more expensive calicos or muslins could be imitated by printing on linen. This encouraged the working classes to wear linen outer garments and had a detrimental effect on the wool trade.

Leather clothing, such as jerkins, shoes and work aprons, also needed to be made. Until Medieval times, skins might have been oiled in order to preserve them. They would have been rubbed with animal fat and then smoked in order to cure them but by the seventeenth century, leather making was unlikely to be undertaken in the home. Leather that was used for clothing normally came from cattle skin but the skins of deer, sheep, horse and goat were also used. Older animals gave thicker, poorer quality leather that was used for footwear rather than clothing. This was processed by tanners, who soaked the skins in oak bark and urine, often for more than a year.

Thinner hides, such as calfskin, underwent a process known as tawing, using alum and oil. This was done by the whittawyers and resulted in a paler, softer leather. The whittawyer would soften the skins by soaking them, scrape them with a scudding knife then dip them in a mixture of alum and water, to which egg yolk, flour, salt and oil might be added. Once dried, the leather might then be dampened with fermented bran and then beaten in order to soften it. The softest leather was produced by soaking it in manure, cold chicken droppings and warm dog manure were favoured. Although leather could be coloured using vegetable or mineral dyes, it was normally undyed.

A great deal of time and effort was required by the seventeenth century housewife, in order to clothe her family. In many stages of the process she would be aided by her children, often quite young children. In general, our Stuart ancestors dressed for practicality rather than fashion or ornament and clothing had to be suitable for the working lives that they led.

Further Reading

Baines, Patricia. *Flax and Linen,* 2003, Shire Publications.

Best, Michael R. (ed.) Markham, Gervase. *The English Housewife,* 1986, McGill-Queens University Press, (1615).

Brooke, Iris. *English Costume of the Seventeenth Century,* 1934, A. C. Black.

Cumming, Valerie. *The Visual History of Costume in the 17th Century,* 1991, Batsford.

Cunnington C.W. & P. *Handbook of English Costume in the 17th Century,* 1973, Faber & Faber.

Durham, James. *The Law Unsealed: or a practical exposition of the ten commandments, with a resolution of several momentous questions and cases of conscience,* 2010, (1676). The section on clothing is available at <<**www.covenanter.org/Attire/durhamondress.htm**>>

Kerridge, Eric. *Textile Manufacturers in Early Modern England*, 1986, Manchester University Press.

Peachey, Stuart. *Clothes of the Common People* (forthcoming), Oxbow Books.

Peachey, Stuart and Hopkins, David. *Dyeing Clothes of the Common People 1580-1660,* 2001, Stuart Press.

Peachey, Stuart ed. *Textiles and Materials of the Common Man and Woman,* 2001, Stuart Press.

Ribeiro, Aileen. *Dress and Morality,* 2003, Berg.

Tortora, Phyllis G. and Merkel, Robert S. *Fairchild's Dictionary of Textiles,* 1996, Fairchild Books.

Waugh, Norah. *The Cut of Men's Clothes 1600 - 1930,* 1987, Routledge.

Waugh, Norah. *The Cut of Women's Clothes 1600 - 1930,* 1994, Faber & Faber.

<<**www.elizabethancostume.net/dyes/dyebib.html**>> Transcriptions of contemporary books on dyeing.

<<**www.madehow.com/Volume-4/Linen.html**>> The linen making process.

CHAPTER 5

Tulips, Topiary, Tradescant and Thyme: gardens and gardening

Available sources of information about gardens of the seventeenth century concentrate on the country house gardens of the wealthy. As the gardening practices of the upper classes were aspired to and adopted in a simplified form by the less well off, it is important to appreciate how their gardens developed. Yet it was the cottage or farmhouse garden that had a crucial role to play in the domestic economy of the majority of households. It is therefore necessary to sift contemporary documentation to try to understand what these gardens would have been like. This is no easy task as cottage gardens were the province of the housewife, most of whom were illiterate and left no record.

Country House Gardens

Until the early sixteenth century, it was the monks who had the horticultural expertise necessary to grow fruit, plants and herbs for both culinary and medicinal needs. Following the dissolution of the monasteries, in the 1530s, much of this knowledge was lost but there was a positive outcome of the dissolution. Those who acquired former monastic land began building manor houses, rather than fortified dwellings;

a style of building that allowed scope for formal pleasure gardens. The ornamental gardens of the rich would be in sight of the principal rooms of the house, whilst the more functional kitchen garden, with its vegetables and herbs, would be hidden from view.

Two things influenced the style of these gardens. Firstly, the revitalising of classical ideas, that was the hallmark of Renaissance thought, extended beyond architecture to impact upon garden design. Gardens were intended to be a reflection of the architecture of the house that they accompanied. The Renaissance also brought increasing education. Books about plants and gardens began to be produced, providing information concerning the style and content of the gardens of the time. Initially, books concentrated on the medicinal properties of plants but as the seventeenth century progressed, greater attention was given to their aesthetic qualities.

The second influence was that of royalty and the aristocracy. A country house garden was a sign of status, wealth and sophistication and those lower down the social scale aimed to emulate the features found in their more wealthy neighbours' gardens. The comparative domestic security and prosperity of the Elizabethan era, together with its better educated and cultured ruling class, provided the opportunity to concentrate on garden making. The Tudor knot garden retained its popularity into the seventeenth century; its low hedges dividing the garden into complex, geometric patterns or knots. Threads of these hedges could be woven under and over themselves. By the 1600s, box, privet and hawthorn were replacing woody herbs such as lavender, hyssop, marjoram and thyme as dividers. Initially the spaces between the knots were not planted, instead being filled with gravel or grass but by the

The knot garden's low hedges divided the garden into geometric patterns.

seventeenth century, gardeners were beginning to plant the spaces. After the Restoration, the French term parterre began to be used to describe this form of garden. From this developed the parterre à l'Anglaise, where the hedges were replaced by turf cut into intricate patterns.

The age of exploration provided opportunities for bringing new species back to England and their acquisition became a vital element of Stuart gardening. Plants that are now common in English gardens, including sunflowers and sweet peas, arrived at this time. Gardeners themselves, such as John Tradescant the elder (1570-1638), began to travel with the express purpose of finding new plants. In 1610, Tradescant was sent to Europe by his employer, Robert Cecil, to acquire specimens for Hatfield House; an iconic garden of the early seventeenth century. Tradescant's purchases included anemones and jonquils, as well as new varieties of fruit trees. Journeys to Russia and the Levant followed. John Tradescant the younger (1608-1662) travelled to Virginia, bringing back plants such as magnolias, phlox and asters.

The mid 1630s' obsession with the tulip is illustrative of the allure of the new plants of the first half of the seventeenth century. Tulipomania, verging on hysteria, saw collectors fixating on the accumulation of different varieties. The random nature of tulip cultivation produced unpredictable results, fuelling the excitement and frustrations of connoisseurs, many of whom acquired specimens to the point of bankruptcy. One variety, 'The Viceroy', was advertised, in a Dutch Bulb catalogue of 1637, at a price of between 3000 and 4200 florins, at a time when a labourer might earn 200 florins a year.

Horticulture and botany became the subject of academic study and the first English botanic garden was created in Oxford, for the purposes of scientific research, in 1620. The garden linked to Edinburgh University followed in 1670. This

'The Viceroy', advertised at a price of between 3000 and 4200 florins.

new, intellectual, attitude to horticulture meant that the propagation of plants became more reliable. The study of the medicinal use of plants was also being taken more seriously. In 1673, the Worshipful Society of Apothecaries of London opened their training garden in Chelsea, focussing on the healing properties of plants. During the first half of the seventeenth century, John Parkinson (1567-1650), former apothecary to James I, was appointed Royal Botanist by Charles I. He produced two influential works on plants and gardens, 'Paradisi in Sole Paradisus Terrestris' (Park-in-Sun's Terrestrial Paradise) in 1629 and 'Theatrum Botanicum' in 1640.

The intricate brickwork, woodwork and plasterwork that characterised Jacobean architecture were reflected in the gardens of the time. To this end, architects, such as Inigo Jones (1573-1652), were increasingly likely to be involved in garden design. Water features and topiary became integral elements of country house gardens. A French poet wrote of 'rosemary, cut out with curious order, in satyrs, centaurs, whale and half-men-horses and a thousand other counterfeited courses.'[1] A description of the gardens at Hampton Court, in 1599, also mentions rosemary as the basis of topiary.[2] William Lawson, writing in 1618, advised, 'your gardener can frame your lesser wood to the shape of men armed in the field, ready to give battle; of swift running grey-hounds, or of well scented and true-running hounds to chase the deer.'[3]

From *The Gardener's Labyrinth.*

The turbulence of the Civil War had an adverse effect on these gardens. Royal gardens and those benefiting from royal support or patronage, became a target for the Parliamentarians. With the restoration of Charles II, in 1660, came not only the peace to enable gardening to resume but also continental influences, that arrived with him from France. Charles himself used the French landscape designer, Andre le Notre (1613-1700), who had designed for Louis XIV. Tree planting was a feature of mid seventeenth century gardening. In this way, the trees that were felled during the Civil War began to be replaced and the long, tree-lined avenues beloved of Stuart garden designers were created.

---

1 Du Bartas, Guillaume de Sallustre; trans. Sylvester, Joseph. *His Divine Weekes and Workes,* 1604.
2 Platter, Thomas. *Travels in England,* 1599, quoted in Jennings, Anne, *Tudor and Stuart Gardens* 2005, English Heritage.
3 Lawson, William *The Country Housewife's Garden* 1983 Breslich & Foss (1618) p. 62.

A rather different continental influence appeared at the end of the seventeenth century, with the accession of William of Orange. These, Dutch inspired, fashions resulted in very formal gardens with large avenues of trees and canals and were not always suited to English terrain. Ornamental gardens of the late 1600s became a fusion of all these styles. Designers, George London (c.1640-1714) and Henry Wise (1653-1738), reflected both French and Dutch forms in their designs. The development of nurseries such as London and Wise's, founded at Brompton Park, Kensington in 1681, gave their contemporaries a ready source of plants. By the late seventeenth century, gardens became more open and vistas and focal points were all important. The advent of the Georgians, in the early eighteenth century, was to bring yet another new style, one of more open gardening. Elaborate formal gardens were however beyond the experience of the average Stuart family.

Of Gathering Flowers

As for the time of gathering them, let the planetary hour, and the planet they come of, be observed, as for the time of day, let it be when the sun shine upon them, so that they may be dry; for if you gather either flowers or herbs when they are wet or dewy, they will not keep.

From Nicholas Culpeper's *Complete Herbal*

Cottage Gardens

For the vast majority of the population, gardens were a necessity and intended to be functional, with any tendency to be decorative merely coincidental. The garden of the farmhouse or cottage was normally the responsibility of the women[4] of the household and was, in essence, a herb garden. It may have contained attractive flowers, such as roses, nasturtiums or gillyflowers[5] but these all had a purpose. Some of the contemporary authorities[6] do suggest that ornamental plants were grown by the yeoman class but most labouring families did not have the time or space to cultivate anything that was purely for show.

Gardens would surround the labourer's cottage or be carved out of farmland on a plot that was as close as possible to the farmhouse. Writers of the time recommended the erection of some form of boundary to provide shelter, or to deter wandering animals; chickens posing a particular problem. Only the reasonably well off could afford a brick or stone wall. Fencing, perhaps of oak, was a cheaper alternative, failing

---

4   William Lawson's *The Country Housewife's Garden*, published in 1618, clearly showed that he expected the gardens of the yeomen farmers to be cultivated by the farmer's wife.
5   Although the Shakespearean 'gillyflower' was the carnation, it was used as a generic term for brightly coloured, sweet-smelling flowers such as carnations, stocks and wallflowers.
6   Lawson, William. *The Country Housewife's Garden,* 1983, Breslich & Foss, (1618), pp. 58-59.

Attractive flowers, such as roses, had a purpose

that a hedge would be grown. Hawthorn was a popular choice for hedges and certainly discouraged livestock; Markham recommended four layers.[7]

A certain amount of preparation was necessary before the garden could be cultivated. A level plot was important in order to prevent the soil being washed away. Although it was acknowledged that some soils were more suitable than others, domestic gardeners had to work with the soils that their locality dictated. Wet areas required the digging of draining channels. On sandy soils, manure, animal and human, could be added; wood ash and rotting wood were also used. Many gardeners kept a comfrey barrel, where the leaves of the comfrey were steeped in water for several weeks, creating an effective, if pungent, liquid fertilizer.

Contemporary sources suggest that, although kitchen gardens did not follow the strict geometric designs of the formal gardens, they were divided into rectangular beds. Particularly on wet soils, these may have been raised beds as Lawson suggests.[8] There is no consensus as to the size of the beds, which no doubt varied, but the three foot wide beds, mentioned by some contemporaries,[9] would have allowed for efficient weeding from each side. The gaps between the beds would be just wide enough to provide access but the need to utilise as much space as possible means that they would probably not have been more than a foot wide. In general, vegetables, such as carrots, onions and peas, would be more likely to be grown in plots, whereas herbs would be planted randomly. Some plants would have been grown in terracotta pots with holes in the bottom, similar to modern flower pots. These are not to be confused with pot herbs, such as rosemary, marigold and mint, that were cultivated for, not in, the pot.

7   Markham, Gervase. *The English Husbandman,* 2008, BiblioBazaar, (1613), p. 214.
8   Lawson, William. *The Country Housewife's Garden,* 1983 Breslich & Foss, (1618), p. 13.
9   Hill, Thomas. *The Gardeners' Labyrinth,* 1577, Henry Bynneman, p. 26.

Lawson advised growing larger plants, such as fennel, angelica and hollyhock against the walls or in borders and low growing plants like marjoram, onions and pansies in the middle of the garden.[10] In the absence of greenhouses, tender plants would be covered with straw or leaf litter in winter, this could be heaped on top of an arrangement of willow twigs. Hot beds were used for plants such as pumpkins and cucumbers. These were constructed in the spring and required fresh horse manure, to a depth of three or four feet. Poles were arranged over the crops and these could be covered with cloths, mats or straw, as protection from the frost.

The metal elements of garden tools would be made by the blacksmith, so the very poor relied on wooden spades and rakes that they could make

Comfrey leaves were steeped in water creating a liquid fertilizer.

10   Lawson, William. *The Country Housewife's Garden,* 1983, Breslich & Foss, (1618), p. 23.

themselves. Wattle hurdles made adequate sieves and wheelbarrows would have been used. Irrigating plots required considerable effort. Rainwater could be collected in barrels but when this ran out, a journey to the nearest spring, well or pump was needed. Thomas Hill described a watering pot, in 1577, as having a 'narrow necke, bigge belly, somewhat large bottome, and full of little holes, with a proper hole formed on the head, to take in the water, whiche filled full, and the thombe layde on the hole to keepe in the aire, may in such wise be carried in handsome manner'.[11] The term watering can was not coined until 1692[12] and thus probably did not resemble the modern watering can until 1885, when a design incorporating a spout and rose was first patented.

Remedy for Worms

Worms may easily be destroyed. Any summer evening, when it is dark, after a shower with a candle you may fill bushels. But you must tread nimbly, and where you cannot come to catch them, so sift the earth with coal ashes and inch or two thickness, and that is a plague to them, so is sharp gravel.

From William Lawson's *The Country Housewife's Garden*

The well equipped cottage garden contained a beehive of wood or straw to provide the family with honey and beeswax; thus giving the Stuart housewife yet another job. Plants such as wallflowers, lavender and borage were important in order to attract the bees and fennel was used to dress the hives for swarms. Whilst bees were beneficial, other insects were a problem for the seventeenth century gardener. Markham suggested several remedies, most of which would have been readily and freely available. Boiling water or ash killed what he calls pismires (ants); chimney soot deterred snails and strong urine was recommended to thwart caterpillars. Planting garlic or onions was believed to prevent moles. Less practical is his suggestion that horses' hooves be burnt to get rid of moths.[13]

Although the wealthy bought in, or even imported, seed, housewives usually harvested their own for use the following year and exchanged seeds with their neighbours. Cuttings or slips could be taken from plants such as rosemary and carnations and roses could be grafted. Incorporated into the superstitions of the seventeenth century was the belief that plants should be sown and harvested in conjunction with phases of the moon. Contemporary accounts disagree about exactly

---

11 Hill, Thomas. *The Gardeners' Labyrinth,* 1577, Henry Bynneman, p. 50.
12 In the diary of Lord Timothy George of Cornwall.
13 Markham, Gervase. *The Second Book of the English Husbandman,* John Norton, (1635), pp. 34-36.

what should be planted or gathered at which time but as a general rule, advice was to sow when the moon was increasing and harvest when it was on the wane. Various herbs were also associated with certain astrological signs. It must be remembered that, in the seventeenth century, there was still a strong correlation between astrology and medicine. For this reason, a herb garden might be divided into twelve to represent the signs of the zodiac and appropriate herbs were grown together; rosemary, thyme, wormwood and cowslip being associated with the star sign Aries for example.

Fennel was used to dress the hives for swarms.

The Use of Herbs

In general, when compared to the modern diet, seventeenth century food was lacking in both variety and strong tastes. The cost of spices put them out of reach of most households, so herbs were used to add interest and flavour. By the seventeenth century, the eating of salads was becoming more popular and a wider range of plants were eaten cold than is common today. Flowers, such as those of the nasturtium, calendula marigold, chive and rosemary could all form part of a salad. Herbal teas were widely used and lemon balm, nettles and camomile were all grown for this purpose, although their role was seen to be medicinal rather than to quench thirst.

Most working households lacked wooden or stone flooring on the lower storey. Compacted mud floors were covered in rushes to absorb cooking fat and animal waste. Strong smelling, strewing herbs, such as lavender and rosemary, would be placed on the

Boiling bluebell bulbs was one of the many seventeenth century recipes for glue.

floor to absorb the worst of the odour. Other garden plants had household uses. For example, boiling the bulbs of the bluebell was one of the many seventeenth century recipes for glue. Some of the plants in the household plot were associated with the production of clothing. Soapwort was used to wash fleeces and teasels provided a method of carding the wool. The garden also supplied the ingredients for dying; St. John's wort producing a red colour and indigo a blue. Camphor was also essential for the prevention of moths.

Although the Stuart labouring family was not overly concerned with personal hygiene, some plants were grown for this purpose. Perfumes could be made from roses or gillyflowers. Thyme was used as a mouthwash and the seeds of wild rocket, when taken orally, were thought to prevent body odour. Lovage would be put in the boots to eliminate unpleasant smells. Rosemary was used in a recipe for tooth soap, along with cinnamon, vinegar and urine.

The fig tree was helpful in the taming of a wild bull.

The seventeenth century was a time of great superstition and magical powers were attributed to some plants. According to Culpeper, the fig tree was reputed to be helpful in the taming of a wild bull.[14] All that was required was to tie the bull to the tree! Stabbing the root of the elecampane, also known as elfwort, rendered the magic of elves ineffective, yet the plant was thought to attract fairies. Herb Bennett, a corruption of Herba Benedicta, was worn as an amulet to ward off evil spirits and venomous beasts. The bay was seen as providing protection from witchcraft and the growing of a bay tree either side of the cottage door was believed to, quite literally, 'keep the witches at bay'. Witches were thought to hide behind the elder tree; for this

14 Culpeper, Nicholas. *Culpeper's Compete Herbal,* 2007, Wordsworth Reference, (1653), p. 115.

> ## Of Sneezewort
>
> The juice mixed with vinegar and holden in the mouth, easeth much the pain of the tooth-ache. The herb chewed and held in the mouth bringeth mightily from the brain slimie flegm.
>
> From John Gerard's *Herbal*

reason it was not to be pruned. If pruning became essential then the witches required an apology. The roots of the mandrake were used as a painkiller but because they were believed to resemble a human being, it was thought they would scream when pulled up and lead to the untimely death of the picker. This problem was solved by tying dogs to the plant and uprooting it in this way.

One of the most important uses of the plants in the cottage garden was as medicines.[15] Several contemporary herbals, such as that of Nicholas Culpeper,[16] describe the uses of each plant in detail. Some of the plants were cure-alls; feverfew was recommended for headaches, freckles and problems following childbirth. Lungwort (pulmonaria) would be used for chest complaints, rue for snakebite and santolina for head lice. Perhaps even more important than keeping the family healthy was dealing with sick livestock. Farriers were often consulted on the treatment of horses but in an age before trained veterinary personnel, animal medicine was largely home grown. Elecampane roots were given to horses; for this reason the plant was sometimes known as horse heal. Sick sheep would be dosed with ground ivy. Herb Robert, on the other hand, was recommended for cattle.

Not only did the housewife have to know how each plant was used but it was her job to ensure that these were available throughout the year by drying or distilling the herbs for use at times when they were not available fresh. She also had to bottle any fruit grown in her garden or orchard and store or dry the vegetables. All in all, the seventeenth century housewife needed to devote a great deal of time and energy to her garden, particularly in the spring and summer. It was essential that Stuart women were skilled in the cultivation, preservation and use of the herbs that they grew. Apart from providing plants for medical and household use, the garden made a vital contribution to the family's food supply.

Further Reading
Culpeper, Nicholas. *Culpeper's Compete Herbal*, 2007, Wordsworth Reference, (1653).
Hill, Thomas. *A most Brief and Pleasaunte Tratyse, Teachynge Howe to Dress, Sowe and set a Garden*, (1563).
Jennings Anne. *Tudor and Stuart Gardens*, 2005, English Heritage.

15   See Chapter 7 for a full account of the medicinal uses of herbs.
16   Culpeper, Nicholas. *Culpeper's Compete Herbal*, 2007, Wordsworth Reference, (1653).

Lawson, William. *The Country Housewife's Garden* 1983 Breslich & Foss (1618).

Mabey, Richard (ed.) Hill, Thomas. *The Gardeners' Labyrinth*, 1987, Oxford UniversityPress, (1577).

Markham, Gervase. *The English Husbandman*, 2008, BiblioBazaar, (1613).

Markham, Gervase. *The Second Book of the English Husbandman*, John Norton, (1635).

Parkinson, John. *Paradisi in Sole, Paradisus Terrestris: a garden of all sorts of pleasant flowers which our English ayre will permit to be noursed up*, 1904, Methuen and Co., (1629).

Parkinson, John. *Theatrum Botanicum: the theater of plants, or, an herball of large extent*, 1640, Thomas Cotes.

Peachey, Stuart. *Farmhouse and Cottage Gardens 1580-1660*, 1996, Historical Management Associates Ltd.

Tusser, Thomas. *500 Points of Good Husbandry*, 1984, Oxford University Press, (1580).

Woodward, Marcus (ed.) Gerard, John. *Gerard's Herbal: the History of Plants*, 1994, Studio Editions, (enlarged and amended edition 1636).

CHAPTER 6

Purges, Plague, Pare and Phlegm: medical practices

Medical Theories and Advances of the Seventeenth Century

Medical principles of the seventeenth century were based on the works of Galen. His theories and anatomical beliefs had been virtually unquestioned for 1500 years. It was dangerous to challenge Galen because his ideas were supported by the church. Illness was seen as a divine punishment and healing could be regarded as interfering with God's plan. The long-held conviction was that the body was composed of four substances, or humours: blood, phlegm, yellow bile and black bile. As soon as the humours became imbalanced the person felt unwell. Medical treatment consisted of trying to re-balance the humours; hence the obsession with blood letting to reduce an excess of blood. Anatomical knowledge was rudimentary, as dissection was frowned upon and many ideas were based on the physiology of animals. Astrology still assumed an importance, particularly in diagnosis and the casting of horoscopes often formed part of a consultation with a physician.

The sixteenth and seventeenth centuries did see medical discoveries and advances. The founding of the Royal Society of Science, in 1660, gave scientists the opportunity to discuss new ideas, many of which were facilitated by the development of microscopes. Pare was a sixteenth century barber surgeon whose battlefield experience led him to apply salves to wounds, in place of boiling oil and to devise artificial limbs. He also developed the use of ligatures for tying blood vessels following amputation. This was more successful than the crude cauterising that was normally practiced however the need for sterilizing the ligatures was not understood, so patients might still die of blood poisoning. Pare was also responsible for discrediting

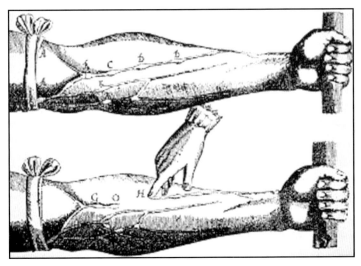

Harvey's ideas met with vehement opposition.

the widely held belief that grasping the bezoar stone[1] was a cure-all for poisons. William Harvey, an anatomist and royal physician to Charles I, contradicted the universally held Galenic theories of circulation and correctly identified the role of the heart and its valves. The invention of the water pump, in the previous century, gave Harvey something with which to compare the action of the heart. Although Harvey received some support from other forward-thinking physicians and anatomists, in general, his work met with vehement opposition. The ideas of Paracelsus (Aureolus Theophrastus Bombastus von Hohenheim) were based on inorganic medicines rather than herbs and Para-celsian theory gradually replaced the Galenic.

The ideas of Paracelsus were based on inorganic medicines.

Much new anatomical knowledge came from the detailed studies of Renaissance artists. Vesalius, a professor of surgery and anatomy, based his extensive anatomical writings on observations. These did perpetuate some of Galen's inaccuracies but Vesalius' works were widely used in the 1600s. The Civil War, in the middle of the seventeenth century, put a great strain on medical services and the increasing use of firearms meant that wounds tended to be more serious than those inflicted in the conflicts of earlier eras. Musket balls were made of lead, a soft metal that spread on impact and thus did a great deal of internal damage; if the victim did not die from the injury, they still had to combat the lead poisoning. The treatment of war wounds did however give surgeons plenty of practice and also helped them to improve their knowledge of anatomy. Despite many innovations and discoveries in the sixteenth and seventeenth centuries, these were treated with caution and even derision, so were very slow to filter down into general medical practice.

Medical Practitioners, their Training and Regulation
Until the Reformation, the responsibility for medical care lay largely in hands of the monasteries. Although monks could be physicians, they could not perform surgery, as a dictat of the Council of Tours of 1163, which was ratified by Lateran Council in 1215, forbade priests from entering the body or shedding blood. This meant that surgery was performed by those with the necessary sharp tools, the barbers.

---

1 Bezoar stones are mineralised hairballs found in the stomachs of animals, usually ruminants and occasionally in humans.

In the seventeenth century, medical provision outside larger centres of population was particularly poor. London had by far the greatest number of physicians per head[2] and Norwich was the next best served. There were also a respectable number of physicians in Bath, supervising those taking the waters. There were few hospitals, with only four to serve London's population of half a million. The scarcity of provincial doctors meant that, despite the poor travelling conditions of the time, physicians journeyed great distances in order to treat patients but this, of course, came at a price. Only the wealthy could afford the services of a qualified, graduate physician although some towns retained the services of a doctor as part of their poor relief provision and a few physicians were willing to treat charity cases. The poor were expected to self-treat and several qualified physicians, such as Thomas Cocke, wrote books designed to make this possible.

There was a distinct hierarchy amongst the medical profession. The physicians were the gentlemen, whereas the apothecaries were the merchants and the barber surgeons, who wielded the tools, were the craftsmen. The physician would have attended grammar school, followed by a classical education at university. At Oxford, doctors studied for fourteen years, whereas the period of study at Cambridge was eleven years. In both cases, students would undertake some practical duties under supervision. The emphasis was on the classical theories of Hippocrates and Galen. Oxford students might get the chance to observe dissections and at Cambridge, the bodies of two criminals were provided annually for this purpose. Knowledge of anatomy was largely acquired by memorising the work of the classical anatomists. The seventeenth century did see the publication of new works by English anatomists such as William Harvey, Francis Glisson and Richard Lower but their ideas were slow to spread. Physicians who trained at European universities might undergo a more

A Snail Water for Weak Children and Old People

Take a pottle of snails, and wash them well in two or three waters, and then in small beer, bruise them shells and all, then put them into a gallon of red cow's milk, red rose leaves dried, the whites cut off, rosemary, sweet marjoram, of each one handful, and so distil them in a cold still, and let it drop upon powder of white sugar candy in the receiver; drink of it first and last, and at four o'clock in the afternoon, a wine glass full at a time.

From W. M's *A Queen's Delight*

---

2 At beginning of the seventeenth century, it is estimated that there were about 500 medical professionals in London. This included physicians, surgeons, apothecaries and other licensed practitioners.

practical training. Those working in London were expected to be members of the College of Physicians (founded in 1518) or they might work under a Bishop's licence. In the provinces, an unlicensed physician would probably escape prosecution. Treatment by a physician was for the rich; the average consultation fee was an angel.[3] Sir Ralph Verney was quite happy to consider giving the doctor plate worth £30 for attending his wife's confinement.

Barber surgeons, practicing within seven miles of London, underwent a seven year apprenticeship that was overseen by the Barber Surgeons' Company, which had been established in 1540. The Company distinguished between the barbers, who were not allowed to perform any operations, apart from teeth pulling and the surgeons who could no

Treatment by a physician was for the rich.

longer cut hair or shave clients. From 1629, the apprenticeship was followed by an examination. Alternatively, surgeons wishing to practice in the capital could apply for a licence from the Bishop of London or the Dean of St. Paul's. Interestingly, in theory, women could also be licensed in this way. Surgeons' Guilds were also found in other principal towns such as Norwich, Exeter, Bristol and York however for the most part, provincial surgery was unregulated and licenses were not required.

The apothecary was supposed to be responsible for the preparation and dispensing of the, primarily herbal, remedies prescribed by the physicians. In practice though, apothecaries also undertook diagnosis and treatment. This was partly a result of the insufficiency of physicians, particularly in areas away from major towns. In 1617, the Worshipful Society of the Art and Mystery of the Apothecaries of the City of London was formed, to regulate those who were working within seven miles of London. Prior to this, London apothecaries had belonged to the Guild of Grocers. Those already practicing in 1617 were automatically incorporated into the Society but newcomers to the profession had to undergo an examination by the master and wardens of the Society. Initial good relations between the Society of Apothecaries and the College of Physicians deteriorated when both sides felt the other was encroaching on their role. Apothecaries resented physicians dispensing and physicians frowned upon apothecaries who provided medicines without a physician's prescription. The quacksalver, a term applied to unlicensed practitioners, was literally one who shouted

---

3   The angel was a gold coin that was initially worth six shillings and eight pence but was later re-valued to about eleven shillings. It was discontinued during the reign of Charles I and from 1663, the standard gold coin was the guinea.

about the ointments,[4] in the market place for example but the epithet quacksalver, or quack, came to be associated with fraudulent medical practice.

Most midwifery in Stuart times was undertaken by local women. There was a system of ecclesiastical licensing for midwives but this was primarily because the church wanted to regulate the baptism of sickly newborns, who were thought unlikely to survive long enough for the vicar to be summoned. Within the guilds, a widow had the right to continue practicing the trade of her late husband, although some restrictions might apply. In practice, women very rarely became professional surgeons or physicians but females, from all classes, were involved in treating their families, neighbours, servants or tenants. Recipe books, letters and diaries of middle and upper class seventeenth century women survive to provide evidence of this. It is likely that this behaviour was similar amongst working women, who had to rely on oral tradition to pass on their knowledge. Male professional physicians were known to have used recipes of lay-women and there was a considerable overlap between the treatments meted out by professionals and amateurs, male or female.

Selected Epidemics

1603 Plague
1625 Plague
1636 Plague in Newcastle
1643 Typhus in Reading
1644 Typhus in Tiverton
1665 Plague
1670 Measles in London
1674 Measles (by the seventeenth century this was distinguishable from smallpox)
1674 Smallpox in Cambridge
1675 Influenza in London
1675 Smallpox in Bath
1681 Smallpox in London and Norwich
1698 Typhus in Bristol
1699 Smallpox in Leeds

Causes of Death and Ill Health

In the seventeenth century, most deaths were caused by epidemic diseases such as plague, smallpox or measles, by accident, or by illnesses associated with poor public health, notably gaol fever (typhus) or the bloody flux (dysentery). Typhus was spread by the body louse, whose ideal habitat is the seams of clothing that is being worn and thus is at body heat. Situations where woollen clothes were not removed for long periods, such as the sieges of the Civil War, were perfect breeding grounds for the louse and typhoid epidemics were widespread in these circumstances. Other common complaints were consumption (tuberculosis), the king's evil (scrofula),[5] gout, kidney stones, worms and ague (malaria), particularly in low lying areas. The French pox (syphilis) was on the increase but there were fewer cases of leprosy than in Medieval

---

4 'Quack' being the Old German and Old Dutch for shout.
5 Scrofula is a form of tuberculosis. It was believed that it could be cured by the touch of the king.

times. Ailments that are now known to be a result of vitamin deficiencies, such as scurvy and rickets, were rife; although there was an awareness of the benefits of lemons for scurvy.

There was recognition of mental illness and whilst the lower classes might be described as mopish, their betters suffered from melancholia and mania. Those with a mental or physical disability were often treated relatively well; although the parents of someone disabled from birth might be stigmatised, as the suffering of the child would be viewed as a God-given punishment for the sins of the parents. In general, the Stuart period was one of comparative tolerance towards those with special needs. It was not until the eighteenth century Age of Enlightenment that there was a striving for physical perfection and the concept of normal was applied to a person lacking in disability.

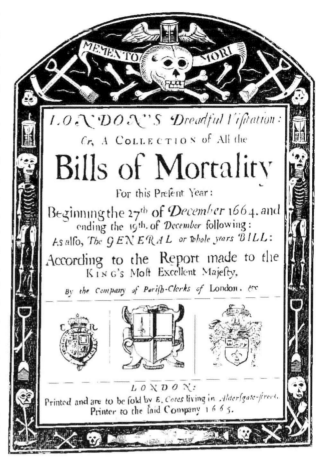

Most of the information about causes of death in the Stuart era comes from London's Bills of Mortality.

Most of the information about causes of death in the Stuart era comes from London's Bills of Mortality. Initially, these were designed to monitor instances of the plague but during the seventeenth century, they listed all causes of death for London and parts of Middlesex and Surrey.[6] It should be noted that these records were complied by parish clerks who recorded some unlikely sounding causes of death, including 'lunatick', 'teeth' and 'horseshoehead'.[7]

Diagnosis

Diagnosis was based largely on astrology, as parts of body were thought to be governed by particular planets. Uroscopy, the examining and tasting of the patient's urine, was often the role of the piss-prophet, although this was beginning to be discredited as a method of diagnosis by the end of the seventeenth century. The practitioner might take a pulse and look for signs of an imbalance of humours. Thus if the patient was hot and sweating an excess of blood might be identified. The body

---

6 These can be found at the Corporation of London Records Office.

7 Horseshoehead appears to have been water on the brain.

The piss-prophet examined and tasted the patient's urine.

might be palpated to locate the site of pain or to detect an abdominal mass. Some physicians still did not feel that they needed to see the patient in person in order to make a diagnosis, although this practice had been banned by the College of Physicians.

Treatments

Treatments for many ailments centred on methods of rebalancing the humours, either by the use of herbal remedies or by more invasive means. Blood-letting could be achieved by cupping, drawing blood off through an area of broken skin, having created a vacuum using a glass cup. Venesection, which had the same effect, involved cutting a vein and collecting the blood in a bleeding bowl. Leeches were still used, though less frequently than in earlier times. Leech collectors were usually female and they would enter a pond, bare legged, hoping to attract leeches that would then be pulled off and stored in a jar to be sold to the medical profession. Purging, using herbal remedies such as fennel, rhubarb or senna, was frequently advised. A seton was a strip of linen or silk that was threaded through the skin and drawn from side to side, on a daily basis. This was designed to encourage pus to leave the body in order to rebalance the humours. With the same purpose in mind, an issue, or small ulcer, might be created using a hot iron or a caustic substance.

The barber surgeon would treat an excess of phlegm by trepanning, an operation that had been carried out since pre-historic times and from which, amazingly, some patients did recover. The scalp would be shaved, the skin cut and peeled back to expose the skull and a hole would be drilled in the patient's head. A small circle of bone would be removed to reveal the brain below. The operation usually took about twenty minutes and the hope was that the surgeon would stop drilling before brain damage occurred. The patient would be asked to return a few days later, when any

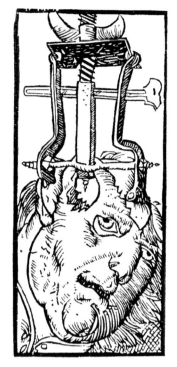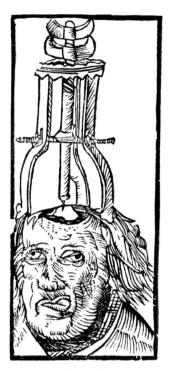

The barber surgeon would treat an excess of phlegm by trepanning.

suppurating matter would be removed using a silver spoon; the surgeons being aware that silver would not react adversely with the brain. Normally a flattened silver coin was put over the hole and the sharpened edges were tapped down so that they gripped into the skull.

Superstition still played a large part in medical prevention and treatment. An example of this was the use of an amulet with 'abracadabra' inscribed on it to ward off the plague. Folk cures, often involving animal parts, were used. A recipe book of the time[8] advises applying the bones of picked herrings to the feet to alleviate a fever. Samuel Pepys wore a hare's foot, a charm that he believed would prevent colic. It was thought that disease could be transferred to an inanimate object and thus disposed of. In this way, a snake would be passed across a swollen neck before being sealed in a bottle. The bottle would then be buried in the belief that the swelling would go down as the snake decayed. Whooping cough sufferers would stand on the beach at high tide so that, as the tide receded, the cough would depart with it. An alternative whooping cough cure was to tie a bag of live spiders round the neck. Warts would be touched with a pebble before the pebble was placed in a bag and lost on the way to church. The finder of the bag would then acquire the wart. Another way in which disease could be purged was for the patient to hold the leg of someone awaiting burial. The illness would be disposed of with the corpse. A sick person could also boil eggs in their own urine. When the eggs were buried, ants would eat them and the illness along with them.

8 *My Lady Rennelagh's Choice Receipts.*

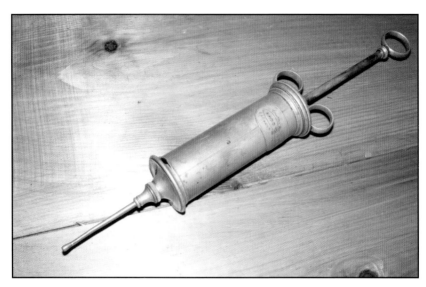

Mercury, administered through a urethral syringe, was the cure for syphilis.

Many seventeenth century treatments sound bizarre, or even downright dangerous, in modern times. A salve for the king's evil required a mixture of salad oil, beeswax and red and white lead.[9] Elderberry and turpentine[10] was to be taken twice a day for a fortnight as a cure for dropsy. Mercury, administered through a urethral syringe, was the cure for syphilis. The mercury might also be inhaled or ingested. Another method was vaporisation, where the patient sat encased in a box, with their head outside. Mercury would be placed in the box and this would vaporise when a fire was lit under the box.

Those suffering from epilepsy were advised to take a mole in the mating season (spring). Male moles were required for female patients and vice versa. The mole was to be dried, powdered and drunk morning and evening for nine or ten days. Markham does acknowledge that this cure might not be fully effective.[11] Moles featured in another cure for convulsions in children. This required a dozen young moles to be disembowelled and their entrails dried. This would be drunk in black cherry water.[12] Frenzy was to be treated by squirting beetroot juice up the nostrils and apoplexy was thought to be prevented by the scent of the fox. Patients afflicted with colic would be given horse dung in wine and snails were considered to be good for tuberculosis. Incontinence sufferers would be encouraged to drink dried kid's hoof

9   Kettilby, Mary et. al. *A Collection of above Three Hundred Receipts in Cookery, Physick and Surgery; for the use of all good wives, tender mothers and careful nurses',* 2010, Nabu Press, (5th edition 1734), pp. 106-107.

10   Obtained by distilling the resin from pine trees.

11   Best, Michael R. (ed.) Markham, Gervase. *The English Housewife,* 1986 McGill-Queens University Press, (1615), p. 15.

12   Kettilby, Mary et. al. *A Collection of above Three Hundred Receipts in Cookery, Physick and Surgery; for the use of all good wives, tender mothers and careful nurses',* 2010, Nabu Press, (5th edition 1734), p. 264.

in beer four or five times a day; a cure which seems more likely to worsen the complaint. Deafness was treated by covering eels in horse dung for two weeks. The oil extracted from the eel would be put in the ears. Sometimes the necessary ingredients were not easy to come by. A cure for the flux (diarrhoea) required dried stag's penis to be grated and added to ale. An alternative was to use the ground jaw and teeth of a pike.

Plague

There were two types of plague. The first, the bubonic, was typified by the swellings or buboes and spread by the bites of fleas found on black rats. Pneumonic plague, on the other hand, was airborne and spread by coughing. The plague returned at regular intervals throughout the seventeenth century although the most famous and most virulent occurrence was that of 1665. It is likely that 15% of the population of London died during this outbreak, one that is believed to have been halted by the Great Fire of London.

The causes of plague were not understood. Some turned to astrology and cited the comet that appeared in the autumn of 1665, together with unfavourable alignments of the planets, as being responsible. Others felt that it was immoral behaviour that was to blame. The most widely held belief was that plague was spread through the miasmas, or bad air, that pervaded towns and cities. Various attempts at prevention were introduced. Examiners were appointed to identify sufferers and guarantee that their houses were shut up and red crosses painted on their doors. Watchmen guarded the houses to ensure that no one entered or left. There was some understanding that a period of quarantine was desirable and those who had nursed plague victims were kept in isolation for a month after the death of the last sufferer. Surgeons and searchers had to confirm that plague was indeed the cause of death and all burials had to be at least six feet deep to contain the infection. They also had to be conducted at night and

Londoners flee the plague.

The plague doctor sported a strange mask.

in the absence of mourners. Public assemblies such as bear-baiting and theatre performances were discouraged. When money changed hands in the market place it would often be put in vinegar, as this was understood to stop the spread of infection. The possessions of sufferers were normally burnt and houses would be lime-washed.

In an attempt to prevent the bad smells being inhaled, pomanders would be carried. As these consisted of oranges with cloves pushed within, both imported items, they were expensive. The cheaper alternative was the tuzzy-muzzy, or bunch of sweet-smelling herbs. The plague doctor, needing to keep his hands free, sported a strange mask with a beak-like feature that would be stuffed with herbs to prevent him inhaling the miasmas. It was the plague that gave rise to the nursery rhyme 'Ring a Ring a Roses'. The 'ring of roses' was the plague spots, the 'pocket full of posies' was the tuzzy-muzzy, or bunch of herbs that would be carried, 'atichoo atichoo' was a sign of the plague and 'all fall down' signified death.

Numerous, largely ineffective, cures were devised for the plague. Roots of the buttercup were recommended and these would be handed to the victim on the end of a stick to ensure that they kept their distance. Gervase Markham lists several herbal cures.[13] One required the patient to urinate on a mixture of yarrow, tansy and feverfew, then drink the strained liquid. Ointment for the plague boils might include a newly slaughtered pigeon, or a mixture of egg yolk, honey and rue.

---

13   Best, Michael R. (ed.) Markham, Gervase. *The English Housewife,* 1986 McGill-Queens University Press, (1615), pp. 12-13.

For the Shingles, a Remedy

Take doves dirt that is moist, and of barley meal heaped, half a pound and stamp them well together. Do thereto half a pint of vinegar, and meddle them together. And so lay it to the sore cold. Lay wall leaves thereupon, and so let it lie three days unresolved. On the third day if need require, lay thereto a new plaster of the same, and at the most he shall be whole within three plasters.

From Thomas Dawson's *A Good Housewife's Jewel*

Dentistry

The barber surgeon was also responsible for dentistry. Every attempt would be made to avoid a visit to the barber surgeon or tooth puller. Various recipes for tooth soaps survive; one involves the use of lavender and ground rats' skulls. The logic being that white teeth required a white ingredient. Urine would be added and the mixture would be applied with a finger or stick. Tooth brushes arrived from France after the Restoration but were slow to permeate down the social scale. Toothache might be treated with spurge, sage or daisy roots and salt.

The seventeenth century belief was that each tooth was inhabited by a worm. As these worms ate their way through the teeth to get to food debris on the surface, a hole would be left. By the time the patient resorted to treatment it is likely that there would be intense pain and swelling and it may have been difficult to be sure which tooth was responsible. The barber surgeon would heat a brass probe and insert it into each tooth to try to identify which one was causing the problem. When the patient screamed, as the nerve was cauterised, the barber surgeon deduced that he had killed the worm.

Tooth pulling was a last resort as it may have resulted in a broken jaw. Before attempting an extraction, the gum would be sliced all round the tooth. The mouth would be held open with a hook, the patient immobilised with the aid of an assistant and the tooth removed with pliers or a pelican. The latter instrument was so called because it was thought to resemble the pelican's beak. The claw was placed over the tooth with the semi-circular metal end resting against the gum. This provided a pivot so that the tooth could be levered out sideways. The rich might aspire to false teeth. These could be made from ivory or bone and were attached to remaining teeth with wires. Ideally, false teeth were real human teeth that were no longer needed. Sometimes servants would be required to provide false teeth for their masters. In the case of the incisors, teeth acquired in this way could be transplanted into the gaps left by newly extracted teeth.

Operations were the preserve of the barber surgeon.

Surgery

Operations were the preserve of the barber surgeon and were not normally carried out by physicians. Seventeenth century surgery was characterised by the lack of antiseptic and anaesthetic. Crude pain relief was administered by the use of alcohol or herbs such as opium or mandrake and occasionally the patient was stunned in order to render them unconscious, a technique not without its own risks. Surgeons preferred their patients to be conscious and ideally screaming, so that they were sure they were still alive. A leather strip would be inserted into the patient's mouth to prevent him from biting his tongue. Burly assistants were essential to hold the patients down during operations. The administering of pain relief, particularly in childbirth, was frowned upon by the church; pain was seen as God given and therefore should not be avoided.

The good barber surgeon was one who worked fast enough for the operation to be completed before the patient died of shock or blood loss. The need for hygiene was unrecognised and it was not until the nineteenth century that surgeons were encouraged to wash their hands between operation and autopsy. Bandages, however bloodstained, were reused and it is thought that the clean and bloody bandages, intertwining as they blew in the wind outside the barber surgeon's tent, gave rise to the red and white barber's pole of modern times. The surgeon's bloody apron was a badge of office, the more blood, the more experienced the surgeon was perceived to be. The problems of bleeding and infection and the lack of pain relief, meant that the survival rate following surgery was probably no more than 30%.

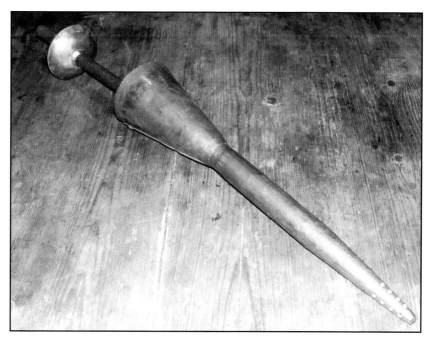

The clyster syringe.

Although germs were not recognised, some of the surgeons' methods did have an antiseptic effect. Bran mixed with honey might be put on wounds and cobwebs were also used for this purpose, funnel webs being the most effective. Instruments were cleaned with wine or urine to prevent rust and this may have had an incidental antiseptic role.

Drinking powdered pigeons' gizzards[14] in white wine was recommended for bladder stones.[15] A less unpleasant alternative was to substitute radishes for the pigeons' gizzards. Unfortunately these 'cures' were rarely successful, so cutting for bladder stones, or lithotomy, was common in the seventeenth century. London hospitals appointed specialist lithotomists. This was an operation that was endured by Samuel Pepys, whose surgery was watched by interested neighbours. Before resorting to surgery, or to provide temporary relief, a probe would be inserted up the urethra in an attempt to dislodge the stones so that they no longer covered the exit to the bladder. This rarely led to a permanent solution, so surgery would be needed. The Celsian method involved inserting a sharp knife up through perineum at the base of the body to pierce the bladder in the hope that the force of escaping urine would expel the stones with it. Often the stones would have to be dislodged with a finger or hook.

An alternative method, known as the Marian or Median technique was developed in the sixteenth century and unlike the Celsian method, could be performed on patients of either gender. This required the stones to be removed using forceps. A

14 According to Mary Kettilby, the amount required was sufficient to cover a shilling.
15 Kettilby, Mary et. al. *A Collection of above Three Hundred Receipts in Cookery, Physick and Surgery; for the use of all good wives, tender mothers and careful nurses',* 2010, Nabu Press, (5th edition 1734), p. 148.

For the Palsy

For the apoplexy or palsy the strong scent or smell of a fox is exceeding sovereign, or to drink every morning half a pint of the dewition of lavender, and to rub the head every morning and evening exceeding hard with a very clean coarse cloth, whereby the humours may be dissolved and dispersed into the outward parts of the body. By all means for this infirmity keep your feet safe from cold or wet, and also the nape of your neck, for those parts it first getteth the strength of evil and unavoidable pains.

From Gervase Markham's *The English Housewife*

grooved stick was inserted through the urethra in order to gain access to the bladder. The urethra was divided using a pair of metal conductors and the passage was dilated until the stone could be extracted. The wound might be cauterised to close it but often a tent was used. This was a rolled piece of bandage, which was inserted into the wound to hold it open and allow the bad humours to escape; in Pepys' case the tent was coated with egg white. Against the odds, although the wound never fully healed, Pepys survived his surgery and each year he held a party to his stone, which was, according to Pepys' fellow diarist Evelyn, the size of a tennis ball. This was of course a real tennis ball, not a modern lawn tennis ball and was about two inches in diameter. There was an unusually high incidence of bladder stones in Norfolk; perhaps this was something to do with the water quality or diet.

Cataract operations were performed in pre-Roman times and changed little in the interim. It was, incorrectly, thought that the cataract was formed by matter descending over the eye like a waterfall, hence the name. Deafness however was normally treated medicinally. One cure for deafness required the patent's urine to be heated in a pewter dish and distilled on to the underside of a second dish that was placed on top. The droplets on the top dish were to be brushed off with a feather and dropped into the ear.[16] The feather was presumably acting as a pipette.

The speculum mondeni, invented by John Woodall, surgeon to the East India Company, was used in cases of severe constipation, common on long voyages where the diet was mainly dried. The rounded end would, if the patient was lucky, be warmed and coated with goose grease. It would then be inserted in the patient, rotated and removed, hopefully bringing with it the compacted matter. The other end of the implement was equipped with a scraper to complete the task. This would allow

16   Kettilby, Mary et. al. *A Collection of above Three Hundred Receipts in Cookery, Physick and Surgery; for the use of all good wives, tender mothers and careful nurses'* 2010 Nabu Press (5th edition 1734) p. 260.

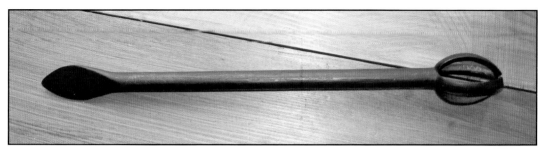

The speculum mondeni was used in cases of severe constipation.

room for the insertion of the clyster syringe, enabling enemas of white wine and honey to be administered.

Battle wounds, such as those inflicted by musket balls, were often fatal. When the wound was to a lower limb, amputation might be possible. Amputation above the knee or elbow was unlikely to be successful because of the associated blood loss. A good surgeon would cut round the limb, down to the bone and pull back the skin and muscle before sawing through the bone. This left a flap that could be used to cover the stump, which would normally be cauterised to close the blood vessels. Sometimes the surgeon inserted two pins through the skin round the stump, and sewed the skin, using a figure of eight, round the pins. The thread could then be tightened gradually until the skin stretched over the stump. Woodall claimed that amputations should not be performed when there was a full moon.

Seeking help from the medical profession in the seventeenth century was both expensive and hazardous; thus ill health was something to be dreaded. Antibiotics and effective anaesthetics were a thing of the distant future and the problems of blood loss and infection remained unresolved. Our Stuart ancestors therefore survived despite, rather than because of, any medical treatment that they may have received.

Further Reading

Best, Michael R. (ed.) Markham, Gervase. *The English Housewife.* 1986 McGill-Queens University Press, (1615).

Cocke, Thomas. *Kitchen-physick or, Advice to the Poor by way of Dialogue,* (1676).

Crawford, Patricia. 'Attitudes to Menstruation in Seventeenth Century England' in *Past & Present,* 91, May 1981, pp. 47-73.

Dawson, Thomas. *The Good Housewife's Jewel,* 1996, Southover Press, (1596/7).

Debus, A. G. (ed.). *Seventeenth Century Medicine in Seventeenth Century England: a symposium held at UCLA in honor of C. D. O'Malley,* 1974, University of California Press.

Kettilby, Mary et. al. *A Collection of above three hundred Receipts in Cookery, Physick and Surgery; for the use of all good wives, tender mothers and careful nurses',* 2010, Nabu Press, (1734).[17]

Lowe, Peter, *A Discourse of the Whole Art of Chyrurgery,* (1654).

---

17 The first edition appeared in 1714.

M., W. *The Compleat Cook* and *A Queen's Delight,* 1984 ,Prospect Books, (1655 & 1671).

MacDonald, M. *Mystical Bedlam: madness, anxiety and healing in seventeenth century England,* 2nd edition, 1983, Cambridge University Press.

Nagy, Doreen G. *Popular Medicine in Seventeenth Century England,* 1988, Bowling Green State University Popular Press.

Raach, John H. *A Directory of English Country Physicians 1603-1643,* 1962, Dawsons of Pall Mall London.

Sloan, A. W. *English Medicine in the Seventeenth Century,* 1996, Durham Academic Press.

Woodall, John. *The Surgion's Mate,* 1978, John Kingsmead Press, (1617).

CHAPTER 7

Primroses, Poultices, Pennyroyal and Pills: the medicinal use of herbs

Preparing the Herbs

Seeking professional medical advice in the seventeenth century was beyond the budget of most families. The physician would tender his opinion, in exchange for a substantial fee and then the herbs required would have to be purchased from the apothecary. Little wonder then that the industrious housewife chose to produce her own simples, or medicinal herbs, in order to cater for the family's medical needs. In doing so she encountered two main problems. Firstly, she needed to know which plant was required for which ailment. All parts of the plant might be used: roots, stems, bark, sap, leaves, flowers or seeds. Herbals, by authors such as Culpeper and Gerard for example, were available in the seventeenth century but most women were not literate. They had to acquire their knowledge aurally and then remember this lore in order to pass it on to their daughters. Herbs were best used fresh but clearly most plants are not available all year round. This gave the housewife her second problem - how to treat the family when the plant she needed was not in season.

Part of a seventeenth century woman's duties included the drying, distilling, or otherwise preserving of herbs so that they could be used throughout the year. Some herbs, such as rosemary and lavender, dry well and cottages would be adorned with drying herbs, usually hung near the chimney. Seeds keep easily and these would be needed to grow crops for the following year as well as being useful in their own right. Dried herbs and seeds would be sewn into folded brown paper

Herbals were available in the seventeenth century.

To Make an Ointment

Bruise those herbs, flowers or roots, you will make an ointment of, and to two handfuls of your bruised herbs add a pound of hog's grease dried or cleansed from the skins, beat them very well together in a stone mortar with a wooden pestle, then put it into a stone pot, (the herb and grease I mean, not the mortar,) cover it with a paper and set it in the sun or some other warm place; three, four or five days that it might melt. Then take it out and boil it a little. Then whilst it is hot, strain it out, pressing it out very hard in a press. To this grease add as many more herbs bruised as before. Let them stand in like manner as long, then boil them as you did the former.

From Nicholas Culpeper's *Complete Herbal*

and stored in a dark, dry place. Alternatively, seeds kept well in wooden boxes or leather bags. The dried herbs could be made into pills by the addition of a little fat to make it easier to create small balls. Dried herbs were also used to make electuaries. This involved grinding the herbs into a fine powder and adding honey before they were consumed. A cataplasm, or poultice, could be made by boiling chopped herbs in water and then adding barley or suet so that it was thick enough to be spread on a cloth that was then applied to the afflicted area. This differed slightly from a plaister; this required the herbs to be mixed with liquid fat, which would then be allowed to harden and could be melted again before use.

A syrup was a liquid medicine that was made by decoction, infusion, or by pressing the herbs with a pestle and mortar to create a juice. A decoction was produced by boiling the herbs in water until the liquid was reduced by about half. The mixture was left to cool and strained through a linen or woollen cloth, before adding a pound of sugar for every pint of liquid. An infusion, on the other hand, involved pouring boiling water on the herbs, covering the pot and leaving them to steep overnight. Again the addition of sugar, dissolved in hot water, was recommended. Sugar was an expensive commodity in the seventeenth century and many ordinary housewives would have omitted this addition, which was to make the medicine more palatable rather than more effective. A julep was of Middle Eastern origin and was usually used as some form of purge. It involved adding the syrup to distilled water; it was consumed straight away, rather than stored.

Some herbs could be distilled. Culpeper writes that distilling in sand was preferable to using a pewter still but gives no details of how this would have been done; 'if I thought it not impossible to teach you the way of distilling in sand by

writing, I would attempt it'.[1] John French's *'Art of Distillation'*, written in 1653, gives more idea and suggests that the sand was used to surround the distillation jars in order to maintain the temperature. Although Culpeper suggested that syrups should be covered with brown paper, distillations were to be kept in pottery jars and covered with a bladder, to keep out the air and prevent evaporation. Most housewives would probably have used an earthenware still, or alembic,[2] for their distillations and this could be covered in cold cloths to aid the process. Products such as lavender water would be produced in this way. Distilled rosemary was recommended as a treatment for a fistula and angelica for infection.

Herbal Cures

When deciding which herb was appropriate, many herbalists and housewives relied on the Doctrine of Signatures or sympathetic magic. This was a like-for-like system that stemmed from the belief that God had created plants with a certain appearance, in order to provide clues as to how they should be used medicinally. A good example of this was lungwort, or pulmonaria, whose spotted leaves were thought to resemble a diseased lung. For this reason, poultices of lungwort would be used for chest complaints. The use of the lesser

Housewives used an alembic for their distillations.

1 Culpeper, Nicholas, Culpeper's Complete Herbal, 2007, Worsworth Editions Ltd, (1652) p311.
2 This was also known as a helm or limbick.

The spotted leaves of the lungwort were thought to resemble a diseased lung.

celandine, commonly known as pilewort, for haemorrhoids, is explained by the appearance of its roots. The greater celandine has a bright yellow sap, therefore it was considered to be beneficial for patients with jaundice. The link between astrology and particular plants was still strong in the seventeenth century. It was advised that the plants be sown and gathered under specific star signs and at the appropriate phase of the moon. For example, the April new moon was the time at which marjoram should be sown.

Sufferers from arthritis were encouraged to beat themselves regularly with stinging nettles. This may seem useful only to take the patients' mind off the arthritis but in fact, it stimulated the white blood cells to reach the site of the pain and thus had a soothing effect. Rue was seen as a poisonous plant, as those with an allergy to rue suffer from a stinging nettle-like rash when they come into contact with it; hence they would 'rue the day' that they touched it. Using the Doctrine of Signatures, rue was prescribed for poisonings, such as snake bite and its efficacy was based on the same principle as the stinging nettle cure for arthritis. Markham suggested mixing the rue with bacon fat to make a salve.[3] Rue was also used as a preventative for typhus, or gaol fever.

There were several herbs that were believed to be beneficial for female complaints. Pennyroyal was helpful for morning sickness and encouraged the flowers, or menstruation. It was also thought to help to expel the afterbirth. Seven berries of the bay would be offered to mothers during childbirth to ensure a speedy delivery. The

3 Best, Michael R. (ed.) Markham, Gervase. *The English Housewife,* 1986, McGill-Queens University Press, (1615), p. 49.

The flowers of the ladies' mantle would be applied to wrinkles.

berries of the cuckoo-pint, which are poisonous if taken in excess, were also given to women in labour in the belief that they would bring forth the child. In earlier stages of pregnancy, the berries provoked a miscarriage and were no doubt used for this purpose. Once the baby was born, fennel would be given for colic and woodbine (honeysuckle) for problems with teething. Even in the seventeenth century, some attempts were made to preserve a youthful appearance. The flowers of the Ladies' Mantle, made into a soap, would be applied to wrinkles and sagging flesh, in the hope of staving off the appearance of old age. This was probably preferable to an alternative moisturiser, used by Mrs Pepys, which involved puppies urine.[4]

For the men folk, mint was the viagra of the seventeenth century, although a convenient antidote was valerian, which had a calming effect. Social diseases were ineffectively treated by chewing on leaves of the soapwort and thyme was applied to testicular swellings. The most useful herb for those fighting in the Civil War was comfrey, known to the soldiers as knitbone or knitwort and believed to heal battle wounds of all kinds. The name comfrey comes from the Latin confervere, meaning to join together and a poultice of comfrey roots was readily applied to broken bones. The plant was most effective if the roots were collected in spring, before the leaves grew, as the roots were fullest at this time. The mashed roots would set to form a plaster. Markham suggests that drinking the juice of the comfrey would also be effective.[5] If the man of the house had over-indulged himself with ale then the remedy

4   The Diary of Samuel Pepys 8 March 1663/4.
5   Best, Michael R. (ed.) Markham, Gervase. *The English Housewife,* 1986, McGill-Queens University Press, (1615).

Marigold Flowers Distilled, Good for the Pain of the Head

Take marigold flowers and distill them, then take a fine cloth and wet in the aforesaid distilled water, and so lay it to the forehead of the patient, and being so applied, let him sleep if he can; this with God's help will cease the pain.

From W. M.'s *A Queen's Delight*

was feverfew, usually eaten on bread. Feverfew was also a cure for headaches. Over indulgence might lead to gout, in which case the berries or roots of the cuckoo pint, would be beaten together with hot ox dung and applied to the affected parts.

The nickname for the buttercup was crazy and a buttercup chain would be put round the neck to prevent madness. It was essential that the buttercups were kept hidden, so they might be covered in hessian. Mary Kettilby records Doctor Wadenfield's remedy for lunacy, which was reported to have cured sixty patients. It involved shredding three handfuls of ground ivy[6] and boiling it in two quarts of white wine. Six ounces of best salad oil were to be added to the reduced, strained mixture. The warm ointment was then to be rubbed on the patient's shaved head. In addition, unspecified fresh herbs were to be bound to the patient's head and three spoonfuls of ground ivy, mixed with beer, were to be drunk each day for ten days.[7] The powdered root of the primrose was considered beneficial for nervous disorders and St. John's wort was prescribed for those with melancholy, or sadness, as indeed it is in the twenty-first century. Wort was an old word for plant and often the first part of the name suggested how it was to be used, as in the case of the lungwort. St. John's wort, however was named for the Knights Hospitallers of St. John, who provided medical treatment during the Crusades.

The queen of herbs, according to Culpeper, was the lemon balm, because of its many uses. The leaves could be rubbed on stings or bites to relieve the itching and when drunk as an herbal tea, it cleansed and revitalised the system. For poor eyesight, it was recommended that the roots and flowers of the primrose were boiled and the film that formed on the surface of the water be applied to the eyelids. For cataract, the greater celandine was advised. A few drops of lavender oil on the bolster at night were thought to induce sleep and relieve snoring. Rosemary was given to aid a failing memory, thus 'rosemary for remembrance' but it was also used as a hair restorative; rosemary remaining an ingredient of many modern shampoos.

---

6   Ground ivy is a member of the nettle family.
7   Kettilby, Mary et. al. *A Collection of above Three Hundred Receipts in Cookery, Physick and Surgery; for the use of all good wives, tender mothers and careful nurses'*, 2010, Nabu Press, (5th edition 1734), p. 177.

The root of the primrose was beneficial for nervous disorders.

Some herbs were specifically used to rebalance the humours. Fennel was thought to counteract a surfeit of phlegm. As the eating of fish was thought to cause an excess of phlegm, fish and fennel were habitually cooked together, to maintain the balance. The seeds, not the bulbs, of the fennel were efficacious for the noxious wind of the belly and the greater celandine sped up the healing of 'old, filthy, corroding and creeping ulcers'.[8] Herb Robert was thought beneficial for old ulcers of the privy parts and hyssop greatly facilitated the expectoration of the mucus.

Many contemporary recipe books recommend mixtures of herbs. Hannah Wolley's plague water required 1lb each of rue, rosemary, sage, sorrel, celandine, mugwort, the tops of red brambles, pimpernel, wild dragon, agrimony, balsm, and angelica. The sheer volume of, for example, 1lb of scarlet pimpernel, is staggering. Once gathered the (of necessity very large) pot was to be filled with white wine and left to steep for four days before distilling.[9] Mary Kettilby's 'Drink for an inward bruise or wound' was even more complex, requiring a handful of each of twenty one different herbs blended in a quart of honey. This was to be taken internally and fortunately, given the trouble involved in its preparation, it lasted 'many years'.[10]

Although many of the cures of the 1600s now seem ridiculous, if it was not thought that they worked, the remedies would not have been tried more than once and no-one would have recorded them for posterity; there would be no point in passing on

8   Culpeper, Nicholas. *Culpeper's Complete Herbal,* 2007, Wordsworth Editions Limited, (1652), p. 64.

9   Wolley, Hannah. *The Compleat Servant-maid: or, the young maiden's and family's daily companion,* 2010, Gale ECCO Print, (9th edition 1719), p. 46.

10 Kettilby, Mary et. al. *A Collection of above Three Hundred Receipts in Cookery, Physick and Surgery; for the use of all good wives, tender mothers and careful nurses',* 2010, Nabu Press, (5th edition 1734), p. 104.

Of the Pimpernel

The floures and leaves stamped and laid upon wounds and ulcers do cure them; but it worketh most effectually being stamped and boiled in oile olive, with some rosin, wax and turpentine added theretoo. Boiled with wine and honey it cureth the wounds of the inward parts and ulcers of the lungs; and in a word there is not a better wound herb, no not tabaco it selfe, nor any other whatsoever.

From John Gerard's *Herbal*

an ineffectual remedy. Whether they acted scientifically or psychologically is another matter. It is important to remember that there are herbal elements in modern mainstream medicines; digitalin, from the foxglove, in heart medicine, for example. In any case, our seventeenth century ancestors had to make use of what was available to them and this was, by and large, the herbal remedies.

Further Reading

Best, Michael R. (ed.) Markham, Gervase. *The English Housewife*, 1986, McGill-Queens University Press, (1615).

Culpeper, Nicholas, *Culpeper's Complete Herbal*, 2007, Wordsworth Editions Limited, (1652).

French, John. *The Art of Distillation*, 1653, E Cotes.

Gerard, John, *Gerard's Herbal*, 1994, Studio Editions Limited, (1633).

Kettilby, Mary et. al. *A Collection of above Three Hundred Receipts in Cookery, Physick and Surgery; for the use of all good wives, tender mothers and careful nurses'*, 2010, Nabu Press, (5th edition 1734).[11]

Minter, Sue. *The Apothecaries' Garden: a history of Chelsea Physic Garden*, 2003, Sutton Publishing Limited.

Wolley, Hannah *The Compleat Servant-maid: or, the young maiden's and family's daily companion*, 2010, Gale ECCO Print, (9th edition 1719).[12]

<<**www.complete-herbal.com/culpepper/preface.htm**>> Alphabetical index of medicinal herbs together with information from Culpeper's Herbal

<<**www.levity.com/alchemy/jfren_1.html**>> Extract from John French's *Art of Distillation*, 1653, Printed by E. Cotes, for Thomas Williams at the sign of the Bible in Little-Britain without Aldersgate.

---

11 The first edition appeared in 1714.

12 The first edition appeared in 1677.

CHAPTER 8

Ducking Stools, Dissenters, Debtors and Drunks: crime and punishment

Matters Affecting Crime

In fact, crime rates were falling during the seventeenth century but rather like today, perceptions of crime were worse than the actuality. This was, in part, due to increased literacy and mass printing that allowed crimes to be reported and publicised via news sheets and pamphlets.

Levels of crime were affected by rising population, increased poverty, the changing prevalent religious and political views and the conflicts that arose from these. There was resentment over what was seen to be unjustified taxation and the gap between rich and poor seemed to be ever widening. Despite the measures of the Elizabethan Poor Law, the view that individuals were to blame for their poverty prevailed. This attitude was fuelled by the Puritan outlook and meant that some were reluctant to help those in need.

Crimes

In 1688, fifty different crimes might attract the death penalty. This number would rise steadily throughout the eighteenth and early nineteenth centuries, giving rise to what was known as the Bloody Code. The concept of severe punishments for what would now been seen as minor offences, was a phenomenon of the 1700s, rather than the seventeenth century.

Many crimes fell into the category of civil offences, transgressions such as diverting water courses and leaving a dunghill in the wrong place were commonplace and these misdemeanours normally came under the jurisdiction of the manorial courts. Crimes against property, such as theft or poaching, were frequently inspired by need, rather than greed. As the property often belonged to the rich, the lawmakers, these were considered to be serious crimes. Debt was often an offence of the middle classes; our poorer ancestors would have found it difficult to obtain credit or loans in the first place.

There was continuing unease and a fear of social unrest. This was exacerbated by the population increase and the displacement of those fighting in the Civil War. Attitudes to vagabondage were influenced by the Puritan view that it was a sin to be idle. The comfortably off were also aware that, under the terms of the poor law, they may be liable for supporting casual wanderers. The settlement legislation of 1662 tightened up the regulations regarding who was responsible for paupers but this just created more ways of falling foul of Justices of the Peace.

Males comprised 80-85% of all seventeenth century criminals. If a woman committed an offence it tended to be less serious; scolding, gossiping, giving birth to an illegitimate child or a minor assault for example. When females were involved in something of greater consequence, it was usually as an accomplice to a male offender. The exception was those accused of witchcraft,[1] where females greatly outnumbered males. The moral climate of the time meant that women were punished more severely than men, for same crime.

Crimes against the church were many and varied. These became more numerous and more severely dealt with under Puritan rule, during the Commonwealth. Non-attendance at church, blasphemy and heresy were punishable by anything from a fine to death. It was also necessary to take communion at least once a year. The laws against blasphemy and adultery were tightened and in 1650, they became capital offences. Seven years later, music and betting were prohibited in alehouses and taverns. The prevailing atmosphere of the mid-seventeenth century saw brothels closed and the number of alehouses reduced. Suicide was regarded as a crime. The body was denied a Christian funeral and instead was buried at the cross roads with a stake through the heart.

The ultimate crime against the church was heresy, which embraced attempts to promote religious doctrines that were contrary to that prevailing at the time. The last person to be burnt at the stake for heresy in England was Edward Wightman, a radical Anabaptist who claimed to be the saviour of the world. He came from Burton on Trent and was put to death in Lichfield market square on the 11th of April 1612. The heretics' fork, more commonly associated with the continent, was used to extract confessions of heresy through sleep deprivation. The metal instrument had two prongs on either end, which were pressed under the chin and into the chest. The

1 See Chapter 9 for a full discussion of witchcraft.

The heretics' fork was used to extract confessions.

victim would be suspended in some way so that they were unable to lie down. As their head dropped forward, the prongs would become more firmly imbedded, thus keeping them awake.

Fears of rebellion by those who did not conform to the Church of England led to a series of laws intended to suppress dissenters of all kinds. These included the Conventicle Acts of 1664 and 1670, which made it an offence to gather in groups of more than five adults for the purposes of worship, unless it was within the Church of England. Dissenters were forbidden from holding offices by the Corporation Act of 1661 and the Test Acts of the 1670s. In addition, the Five Mile Act effectively prevented a non-conformist minister from entering a large centre of population or an area where they had preached in the past. Some of these restrictions were lifted by the Toleration Act of 1689 but our Stuart ancestors were still obliged to obey the laws of both church and state.

Punishments

At the family level, behaviour was regulated within the home by the man of the house. Corporal punishment of children was the norm and husbands were also expected to control the behaviour of their wives. Whilst not enshrined in the statute books, folklore held that, according to the 'rule of thumb', any stick used for beating a wife must be no thicker than the man's thumb. The first stage of correction for a gossiping or nagging wife was to cut her hair short. The advantage of the coif was that a woman thus punished could hide her shame from her neighbours. If this did not work then the Scold's Bridle would be applied. This iron cage was fastened over the head, with a metal plate inserted into the mouth to prevent the tongue from moving. Some of these plates had spikes underneath, making moving the tongue even more hazardous. Although breathing was not impeded, it was impossible to talk. A chain would be attached to the bridle and the woman would be paraded round the village, to shame her in front of her neighbours.

Public humiliation had an important role to play in seventeenth century punishments. Many sentences were carried out where they could be viewed by all and act as a deterrent. The market place or village green was an ideal position for the pillory. This restrained head and wrists so that the offender was forced to assume a slightly stooped stance. Bearing in mind that the average sentence was six hours, this was a very painful position to have to hold. He, or more rarely she, would have to face not only the discomfort but also the elements and whatever his fellow citizens decided to throw at him. Bad fruit, eggs, stones or the contents of the chamber pot would suffice, although the stereotypical tomatoes would be unlikely; as a recent import they would have been far too expensive. Stinging nettles, holly or teasels could also be applied to tender parts of the anatomy. The punishment might be tailored to fit the crime. So someone who had been found selling rotten fish would have his wares burnt under his nose. If the

The scolds' bridle would be applied to a nagging wife.

public disapproved of the punishment they might throw flowers instead of missiles; this was most common in cases of sedition. To ensure that the victim did not escape, their ears would be nailed to the pillory. Once they were let out, they would be 'ear-marked' as a criminal for evermore. The type of offences that might result in time in the pillory included drunkenness, selling underweight or rotting produce and cheating at cards.[2]

Fines were imposed for such things as profanity, non-attendance at church and gambling. For most of our ordinary ancestors, the sums required were prohibitive. The non-payment of fines would result in an alternative, physical, punishment. The stocks were similar to the pillory and were often the sentence when a fine remained unpaid. They restrained the seated offender by the wrists and ankles and again the criminals were a target for both missiles and ridicule.[3]

The village green was an ideal position for the pillory.

2   At times during the seventeenth century, the playing of cards was itself an offence.
3   The pillory was abolished in Britain in 1837 and the stocks in 1872.

The offender in the stocks was a target for both missiles and ridicule.

The church embraced the con-cept of humiliation as a form of punishment by insisting on public penance, normally during the Sunday service. This often followed crimes of a sexual nature, such as adultery, fornication or the bearing of an illegitimate child. Apostasy, the abandoning of prevailing religious doctrines, was also punishable by public penance. Some churches had stones by the door where the penitent sat. Alternatively, the offender might be expected to prostrate themselves before the font. Penance might be accompanied by the need to dress distinctively, in anything from sackcloth and ashes to a white shift.

The ducking-stool was not, as is popularly perceived, the punishment for witchcraft but for scolds. The scold, normally a woman, would be tied to the wooden seat, on the end of a long pole, and immersed in the village pond. Whipping was often the sentence for vagrancy or theft. Until the latter years of the seventeenth century, this too would be a public punishment. The criminal was tied to the back of a cart and whipped through the streets until blood was drawn.

Archbishop Laud's Form of Penance and Reconciliation of a Renegado or Apostate 1635

He is to stand at all time of divine service and sermon in the forenoon in the porch of the church ... in a penitent fashion in a white sheet, with a white wand in his hand, his head uncovered, his countenance dejected, not taking any particular notice of any person that passeth by him; and when the people come in and go out of the church, let him upon his knees humbly crave their prayers and acknowledge his offence in this form, 'Good Christians, remember in your prayers this poor apostate or rene-gado.'

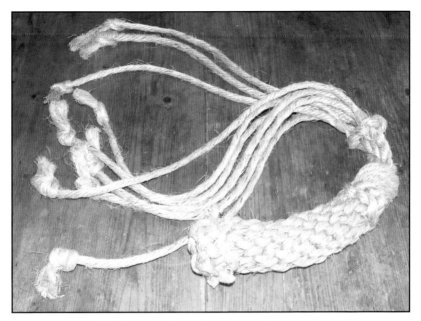

Whipping was often the sentence for vagrancy.

Prisons and parish lock-ups were used primarily to hold those awaiting trial, rather than as a punishment. Under the terms of the Elizabethan Poor Law, vagrants or runaway apprentices might be held in the House of Correction. The main exceptions were witches and debtors, who were normally imprisoned; London's Fleet being the most notorious debtors' prison. Conditions in all prisons were poor and could only be improved if the prisoner had money and friends on the outside. Money changing hands might encourage the warders to provide fuel and reasonable food, or to allow visitors.

In the seventeenth century, the death penalty was reserved for serious crimes such as murder, treason, arson, or counterfeiting. Treason could be high treason, for crimes against the monarch, or petty treason for the murder of a superior; thus a woman who killed her husband would be committing petty treason. The death penalty for men would normally involve hanging, drawing and quartering. Having been dragged to the execution site, the prisoner was choked but not killed. Then they were mutilated whilst still alive. A skilful executioner could keep his prisoner alive whilst the intestines were pulled from the body and burnt. The body was then quartered and distributed around the town to deter prospective criminals. Hugh Peters, the chaplain with Cromwell's New Model Army, was hung, drawn and quartered for regicide, after the Restoration. A less serious offence might result in hanging only. The nobility were entitled to the more civilised beheading; Charles I being the most famous beheading of the seventeenth century.

Murderers might be hung in chains near the site of their crime. It was not considered seemly for women to be hung, drawn and quartered as this would mean her naked body was in public view. Instead, women found guilty of treason would be burnt at the stake. Pregnant women could 'plead their belly'. Women from the

The nobility were entitled to the more civilised beheading.

courtroom would be chosen to check that the accused was indeed pregnant. This was normally done by looking for signs of movement, so would not help in early stages of pregnancy. If shown to be pregnant, the woman's sentence would be delayed until after she had given birth. In practice, this might lead to a reprieve as a motherless child would be likely to be a burden on the parish. Transportation could also be substituted as a punishment.

Transportation to North America and the West Indies began in 1615 as a way of circumventing the need for the death penalty. Those who had been reprieved following a death sentence would be transported for fourteen years, with seven year sentences for less serious crimes. The system was formalised in 1662, when exile became illegal as a form of punishment under the terms of the Habeas Corpus Act. Instead, a system of conditional pardons was devised, whereby the pardon was issued providing the offender agreed to remove himself from the country for a specified time. There were no transport ships. Transportees were purchased from the sheriff by merchants. The money that changed hands was to cover the amount owed to the jailor and clerk of the court, who would have to draw up a pardon. Once across the Atlantic, the merchant had the right to sell the offender as an indentured servant for the term of their sentence. This was clearly more profitable for the merchant if the criminal was strong and fit. Those whose sale was unlikely to recoup the costs, languished in jails indefinitely awaiting transportation. The other problem with this system was that colonies began to prohibit the importation of convicts. Virginia issued a ban in 1670, followed by Maryland in 1676. From 1697, Jamaica refused to allow female transportees to enter.

The greatest and most grievous punishment used in England for such as offend against the State is drawing from the prison to the place of execution upon an hurdle or sled, where they are hanged till they be half dead, and then taken down, and quartered alive; after that, their members and bowels are cut from their bodies, and thrown into a fire, provided near hand and within their own sight, even for the same purpose. Sometimes, if the trespass be not the more heinous, they are suffered to hang till they be quite dead. And whensoever any of the nobility are convicted of high treason by their peers, that is to say, equals (for an inquest of yeomen passeth not upon them, but only of the lords of parliament), this manner of their death is converted into the loss of their heads only.

From William Harrison's *Description of Elizabethan England*

The clergy and upper classes were able to earn a reprieve through a system known as the benefit of the clergy. Initially this was open to those associated with the church but by the seventeenth century, any man who could read was able to claim. This entitled them to be tried in the ecclesiastical courts, where sentences were less severe, rather than the secular courts. The most serious offences such as murder, burglary, rape and theft from a church were not eligible for benefit of the clergy in the 1600s.

Women were not able to claim benefit of the clergy on the same terms as men until 1691. Although females who had stolen goods worth less than ten shillings could claim from 1623/4, for men the limit was forty shillings. The passage from the bible that the accused was asked to read was usually from Psalm 51 and this became known as the neck verse, as the criminal's neck might be saved. Of course it was perfectly possible for an illiterate offender to recite the necessary passage by rote. If the court felt that the death penalty was well deserved or if the judge was particularly harsh, higher levels of literacy might be demanded and other verses would be required. The benefit of the clergy could only be claimed once. Those who received it were branded on the thumb, so that they could be identified. The letter used reflected the crime; 'f' for felon, 't' for theft and so on. This was applied, in public, in the courtroom.

Branding was also used as a punishment in its own right. In 1656, James Naylor, a renegade Quaker, spent time in Exeter jail for vagrancy. Following his release, he was accused of impersonating Christ in Bristol. His punishment was to be branded on the forehead with a 'b' for blasphemer, his tongue was pierced with a red hot iron and he was pilloried before being imprisoned.

Law Enforcement

In the seventeenth century, control was maintained through the deterrent value of strict punishments. A professional police force was seen as expensive and unnecessary. Unpaid parish constables were appointed to work under the Justices of the Peace. Their duties included dealing with vagabonds, accompanying individuals who were being removed under settlement legislation and apprehending putative fathers in bastardy cases. They also supervised the village lock-up and organised the hue and cry. The hue and cry required bystanders to raise the alarm, search for and pursue offenders, making as much noise as possible. The offering of rewards also encouraged the public to turn detective. The thief takers capitalised on this system by attempting to make a living from seeking out criminals and collecting the rewards. In the towns, watchman and sergeants patrolled the streets dealing with drunkenness and imposing market regulations.

In cases of serious unrest, the militia could be called in. By the 1600s, these trained bands were organised by the lord lieutenants of each county and were intended to have a defensive role, quelling riots and countering threats from abroad. In the mid-seventeenth century, the trained bands formed the basis of some of the regiments of the Civil War.

From Old Bailey Proceedings Online 6th September 1677

A Man married about 10 years ago to a Woman in the Country, having about 3 year since married another at Aldgate (the first being still living) was for the same Arraigned: His first Wives Sister proved the first Marriage, and that they lived together and had two Children. The second Wives Father and Mother proved their Daughters Marriage to him, and that he had a Portion, which was consumed, &c. He had little to say for himself, but being found Guilty, craved the benefit of his Clergy, and by special Order hath Squire Ketches Arms very fairly engraven in his Hand.

Courts

As well as being responsible for matters that were related to misdemeanours, manorial courts ensured that the customs of the manor were upheld. By the seventeenth century, this was primarily the role of the Court Baron, as the Court Leet was in decline. The offences were of a civil, rather than a criminal nature, with presentiments for trespass, slander and minor damage being common. Punishment was normally by way of an amercement or fine.

The church courts were often referred to as the bawdy courts, because of the nature of many of the offences that they tried; accusations of fornication, adultery and bastardy for example. There was a hierarchy of these ecclesiastical courts ranging from the archbishops' courts, to those of the bishop and the archdeacon. Each court could try offences that took place within its own area. In some places, courts known as peculiar courts also had jurisdiction. An appearance in an ecclesiastical court brought not only punishment but the disapproval of the community for the moral transgression.

The principal upholders of the law, in the civil court system, were the forty or so Justices of the Peace who were appointed for each county. The qualifications needed to be a Justice of the Peace remained unchanged for three hundred years and in 1689, they were still required to be 'the most sufficient knights, esquires and gentlemen of the law, resident in the county and owning an estate worth not less than £20 per annum'. When they took their commission, normally at the beginning of each reign, a Justice had to agree to 'keep and cause to be kept all ordinances and statutes for the good of the peace, and to chastise and punish all persons that offend against the form of the ordinances and statutes.'[4]

---

4   Statute 13 Richard II c. 10. 1388.

The secular courts had their own hierarchy, with the minor cases being heard at the Petty Sessions, which were held on a regular basis, perhaps at the local inn. The Justices of the Peace conducted the majority of trials during the Quarter Sessions, which met, as the name suggests, every quarter, in market towns or cities. The exception was Middlesex where the Quarter Sessions only convened twice each year. If the case was too serious for the Quarter Sessions to pass judgement, it would be referred to the Assize Courts. These were presided over by a team of itinerant judges, visiting each county two, or occasionally three, times a year. Cases of murder, highway robbery, recusancy and forgery all might be tried by the Assize judges. At the Old Bailey, the court that covered London and Middlesex, during the seventeenth century, the Lord Mayor acted as chief judge.

It would be unusual for the lives of our Stuart ancestors not to be touched by crime in some way; whether as victims, witnesses, lawbreakers or law enforcers. It is only right that we should try to understand how they would have been regarded and treated by their contemporaries, in which ever of these roles they found themselves.

Further Reading

Atherton, Ian and Como, David. 'The Burning of Edward Wightman: Puritanism, prelacy and the politics of heresy in early modern England' in *English Historical Review* vol. 120, issue 489, December 2005, pp. 1215-1250.

Chapman, Colin. *Ecclesiastical Courts, their Officials and their Records,* 1992, Lochin Publishing.

Dalton, Michael. *The Countrey Justice: conteyning the practise of the justices of the peace,* 2004, The Lawbook Exchange Ltd., (1655).

Harrison, William. *Description of Elizabethan England*, 1877, The New Shakespeare Society, (1577-8).

Hawkings, David T. *Criminal Ancestors*, 2009, The History Press.

Jacob, Giles. *The Compleat Court Keeper* 1713 Bernard Lintot & Thomas Ward.

Sharpe, J. A. *Crime in Seventeenth-Century England: a county study*, 2008, Cambridge University Press. A study of the county of Essex.

Sharpe J. A. *Crime in Early Modern England: 1550-1750 (Themes in British Social History)*, 1998, Longman.

Tarver, Anne *Church Court Records: an introduction for family and local historians* 1995 Phillimore and co. Limited.

<<**http://www.oldbaileyonline.org/**>> Indexed Proceedings of the Old Bailey 1674-1913. This site also includes an article on punishments.

<<**http://www.localhistories.org/pun.html**>> A description of various historical punishments.

CHAPTER 9

Superstition, Sorcery, Sabbats and Spells: witchcraft

Even in modern times superstition remains. We still touch wood, refuse to walk under ladders and throw spilt salt over our shoulders. These are remnants of an age when such rituals held much greater significance and formed part of a way of life. Few of our ancestors were directly involved in witchcraft trials, either as the accused or the accuser, but all of our seventeenth century forbears lived in a world where there was an underlying belief in, and fear of, witchcraft. Under normal circumstances, the likelihood of bewitchment would not have been uppermost in their minds. In times of trouble however, a supernatural cause would be assumed and folk might look at their neighbours, seeking someone upon whom to pin the responsibility for their misfortune. Macfarlane reminds us that witchcraft was 'a normal part of village life, widespread and regular.'[1] We owe it to our ancestors to try to comprehend the prevailing atmosphere of Tudor and Stuart times; an atmosphere that could escalate into mass hysteria and persecution.

The Tenets of Witchcraft

The central role of religion in the lives of our Stuart ancestors helped to shape their conception of witchcraft; a phenomenon that was very different from the modern, pagan religion Wicca. Not all seventeenth century witchlike activity entailed maleficia, or actions with evil intent. Witches could be involved in fortune telling, finding lost objects, herbalism and the faith healing of humans and animals. More sinister pursuits included devil worship, causing illness, death and disasters, such as extreme weather or crop failure. Ill-wishing or bewitching, causing evil spirits to possess another person, were also facets of witches' behaviour.

Witchcraft was closely associated with heresy, as witches were supposed to have made a pact with the devil in exchange for their magical powers. They were left with devil's marks, marks that would not bleed when pricked, as signs of subjugation to the devil. These marks, or teats, were used to suckle their familiars. Familiars were demons in animal form, often cats, dogs, goats or toads, although they could also be invisible. In 1398, the academics at the University of Paris, following debate, ruled that witches were committing idolatry and that all maleficia was heresy. Necromancy on the other hand was the magic of the ruling classes. Necromancers commanded and conjured demons, whereas witches obeyed them. Thus the behaviour of the necromancer, whilst being suggestive of heresy, was not unequivocally the action of a heretic.

---

1   MacFarlane, Alan. *Witchcraft in Tudor and Stuart England: a regional and comparative study,* 1970, Routledge, p. 30.

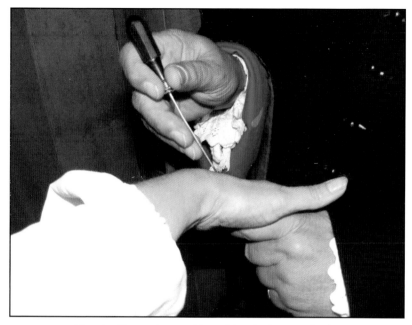

The devil's marks would not bleed when pricked.

The belief that witches flew at night has its origins in the cult of the goddess Diana. Night flight was largely a continental phenomenon and was never considered a crime in England. Surviving recipes for flying ointment contain hallucinogens, like henbane, aconite or belladonna, that can make those who take them believe that they are flying; hence the modern word trip for a drug induced experience. Sabbats, night-time meetings of witches, were thought to involve devil worship, excessive and abnormal sexual practices, cannibalism and infanticide. Traditionally, sabbats took place on a Thursday and the two most important nights of the year were the 30th of April, Walpurgisnacht and the 31st of October, Halloween. The sabbat required witches to work as a group and this led witch trials to focus on the search for accomplices. This, in turn, resulted in chains of accusations and fuelled suspicion and mass hysteria. Like night-flight, sabbats and orgies were tenets of European witchcraft and were infrequently part of British witchcraft trials.

Counteracting Witchcraft

Many took precautions to protect themselves from witchcraft. Witches were thought to exercise their powers through an object; so they needed to obtain a possession from their intended victim, or to leave something of theirs in the victim's house. For this reason, people were reluctant to lend items to, or borrow from, a suspected witch. Avoidance was the best policy; keeping a low profile and taking care not to upset likely witches by refusing their requests for charity. Leading a pious and prayerful way of life was also believed to reduce the likelihood of bewitchment. Various charms, such as stones with holes in, were thought to be helpful. Many amulets had religious associations. Holy water, communion wafers and the wearing of passages of scripture round the neck, specifically the first chapter of John's gospel, were popular. Some plants were also associated with protection from witch-craft. These included rue, also known as herb of grace or herb John and bay. The wearing of red, the colour of Christ's blood, was also thought to have protective powers. Witch bottles, or bellarmines, usually made of grey stoneware, seem to have been seen as a way of warding off evil. Those that have been found by archaeologists tend to be at the exits of properties such as under thresholds or in hearths. Many contain hair, urine, pins or fragments of bone.

Once the witch had activated her curse or enchantment, it was necessary to find a cure or antidote. Fire was believed to be effective, particularly burning an animal. This was perhaps an echo of biblical sacrifices. It was important to identify the witch and get her to withdraw her power and lift the curse. Setting fire to the bewitched item or burning something belonging to the suspected witch was thought to make them appear and thus be a sign of their guilt. To this end, those who believed themselves bewitched would deliberately burn their own hands or feet.

Cunning folk, wise women or white witches, acted as finders of lost property, provided charms or herbal remedies and advised on the causes of affliction. They were important in the identifying of witches and curing the bewitched. They might use a crystal or looking glass and usually consulted good angels, the equivalent of the black witch's familiar. In fact they frequently confirmed a suspicion that the client had already voiced. Those contacting cunning folk were encouraged to make a return visit, thus giving the wise woman the chance to listen to local gossip, find out who had a possible grievance against her client and thus identify a likely witch. It is difficult to tell how many cunning folk genuinely believed in their own powers and how many were deliberate frauds. Combining elements of the herbalist, the faith healer, the medium and the fortune teller, they ran the risk of being accused of maleficium themselves.

Witch Finders

Although they identified witches, the cunning folk were not witch finders. The witch finder specifically sought out witches in return for money. 1486 saw the publication of the witch hunters' manual 'Malleus Maleficarum' (The Hammer of the Witches) but

Matthew Hopkins was a notorious witch finder.

this was not translated into English until long after the witch craze. Two of the most notorious English witch finders were Matthew Hopkins and John Stearne, who were responsible for the Essex witch hunts of the 1640s. Witch finders were aided by, normally female, searchers who examined suspects for the devil's marks, which were thought likely to be hidden in intimate places. There were also watchers who would observe the suspect, usually overnight, to see if they were visited by familiars.

There were critics of the witch finders' work. In 1646, clergyman, John Gaule, wrote *'Select Cases of Conscience Touching Witches and Witchcraft'*, condemning Hopkins and Stearne. Hopkins published his own rebuttal, *'The Discovery of Witches'*, the following year and Stearne did likewise in 1648.

Witchcraft Legislation
The first, short-lived, statute against witchcraft in England lasted from 1542-1547 and was rarely invoked. Prompted by government anxieties and fears of treason, the act was replaced, in 1563, by an *'Acte Againste Conjuracons Inchantments and Witchcraftes'*.

Possible crimes included causing injury or death by witchcraft, invoking evil spirits and using witchcraft to search for missing items or treasure. Causing death or conjuring evil spirits were capital offences but a first offence of causing injury or searching for treasure attracted a one year prison sentence and the offender was required to 'once in every Quarter of the said Yere, shall in some Market towne, upon the Market Daye or at such tyme as any Fayer shal bee kepte there, stande openly upon the Pillorie by the Space of Syxe Houres, and there shall openly confesse his or her Erroure and Offence'. The minimum sentence for a second offence was life imprisonment. There were also punishments for intending to cause death or injury and for using love charms.

In 1604, another era of political instability, James I passed a new act that made death the punishment for a second conviction. A first offence in cases where harm had resulted, or if a body had been exhumed with magical intent, also attracted the death penalty. In addition, the act punished 'aydes, abettors and councellors', something that made association with known witches all the more dangerous. Initially, James I was vehemently anti-witchcraft, publishing *'Daemonologie'* in 1597, setting out his views. In later years however he became less dogmatic. The 1604 act remained on the statute books until 1736, by which time formal prosecutions had long since ended. The legislation that repealed the 1604 act did so in a prevailing atmosphere that believed witchcraft to be impossible. As a consequence, anyone claiming to have magical powers was deemed to have committed fraud and was still liable to punishment.

Persecutions

'Witch-hunts involved not just savage persecutors tormenting innocent scapegoats, but ordinary neighbours with a close affinity to one another who also happened to believe in witchcraft powerfully enough to act out their most violent fantasies.'[2] The stereotypical witch was ugly, often with warts or facial moles but when the surviving documents about specific trials are consulted, it seems that behaviour and demeanour were more likely to lead to persecutions than appearance. Witches were almost always female and often past the first flush of youth. Perhaps menopausal women were more likely to exhibit irrational or eccentric behaviour. Witch and accuser were usually neighbours and well known to each other. Witches were often of lower social status than the bewitched; allegations frequently coming after requests for employment or alms had been refused.

Swearing or blasphemy could lead to accusations of witchcraft, as, conversely, did acts of extreme piety. Witches were known to take communion frequently so that they could appropriate the bread and wine, which was then used for magical purposes. There was considerable poverty and hardship in the sixteenth and seventeenth centuries and foodstuffs that would normally be rejected were being eaten. This included rye that was infected with the toxic fungus, ergot. Ergot could cause fits, paralysis and hallucinations; victims often believed that their skin was being torn or

2   Gaskill, Malcolm. *Witchfinders: a seventeenth century English tragedy,* 2005, John Murray, p. 286.

pricked. It was a small step from this to a sufferer claiming that they were being bewitched.

It was only possible to witness the effects of witchcraft, not the act itself. Therefore accusations were based on a discussion of motives and reports of the consequences of alleged bewitchment. Indications of witchcraft included cursing someone who subsequently suffered illness or bad luck, associating with a known witch, being implicated by another witch, having an unnatural mark or entertaining familiars. Several of these 'strong presumptions' were regarded as sufficient to assume guilt.

Dalton's manual for Justices of the Peace, published in 1618, emphasised the need to seek information on the character and family of all suspected felons. He advised the justices to investigate, 'his parents, if they were wicked ... His nature, if civill or hastie, wittie or subtle, a quarreller, pilferer, or bloudie minded... His

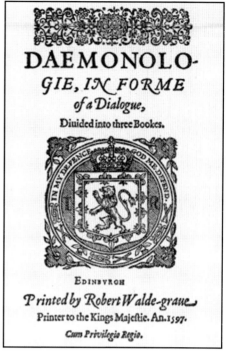

DAEMONOLO-
GIE, IN FORME
of a Dialogue,
Diuided into three Bookes.

EDINBVRGH
Printed by Robert Walde-graue
Printer to the Kings Majestie. An.1597.
Cum Privilegio Regio.

James I published 'Daemonologie' in 1597.

trade; for if a man liveth idly or vagrant ... it is good cause to arrest him on suspicion.... His companie....His course of life; if a common alehouse haunter, or riotous in dyet, play or apparrell. Whether he be of evil fame or report.'[3] These recommendations took on particular significance during witchcraft prosecutions. In cases of witchcraft, witnesses would be allowed who were inadmissible in trials for other crimes; for example minors could give evidence, as could the spouse of the accused. Dalton also advised that 'half proofes are to be allowed' in accusations of witchcraft. Confession was regarded as irrefutable proof. Confessions extracted under pressure were supposed to be ratified the next day, without the use of torture, before they could be accepted.

It was possible to be tried by the ecclesiastical or the secular court system. There are instances of individuals who were tried in both but it is not clear if these were a result of different accusations. As far as the church was concerned, accusations were usually made on the basis of common fame, in other words, rumour. 'Witchcraft suspicions tend to move in an ever-widening ripple through the village, the final accusation being based on a general consensus of opinion which rested on the mutual exchange of fears through gossip.'[4] It was possible to get a charge of witchcraft dropped if the accused went through a process know as purgation. They were required to swear their innocence and persuade three or four others to testify as to their good character. Popularity with ones neighbours was therefore critical. If the

3 Dalton, Michael. *A Countrey Justice,* 1618, p. 266.
4 MacFarlane, Alan. *Witchcraft in Tudor and Stuart England: a regional and comparative study,* 1970, Routledge p. 110.

accused was not able to purge, or admitted their guilt, then the next stage was public penance, involving confession, a promise to reform and frequently the payment of a fine. Penance was normally part of the regular Sunday service and the penitent would wear a white robe and carry a white wand.

Punishments

Although witches might be tried in a church court, in England, witchcraft was essentially a secular crime, associated with bewitching rather than heresy. Officially, torture was only allowed in cases of treason and the capital sentence for witchcraft was hanging; considered to be a lesser punishment than burning,

Some Notable Seventeenth Century English Witch Trials

1612 Pendle Forest, Lancashire
1612 Northamptonshire
1645 Yarmouth, Norfolk
1645-6 Essex
1652 Maidstone, Kent
1664 Somerset
1673 Northumberland
1682 Bideford, Devon

which was favoured on the continent. The ducking-stool was the punishment for scolds not witches. The confusion arises because of the practice of swimming witches; tying the left thumb to the right big toe and vice versa before they were thrown in a pond to see if innocence could be established by the accused sinking. Trial by water dates from ancient times but had been forbidden by the Pope and by the laws of the church. Stearne claimed that he only swam those who asked for this trial, in other words those who presumably sought incontrovertible evidence of innocence.

The pear of anguish expanded to cause extreme pain.

Punishments were not supposed to involve drawing blood, maiming or death. For this reason most relied on a form of crushing, although how this could be seen to not comprise maiming is hard to understand. These punishments could also be used to extract confessions. Some of the more gruesome methods included thrawing, twisting ropes round the head, the pinniewinks or thumbscrews and bootikins, leg braces that were hit with a hammer in order to tighten them. In addition, nails were ripped out and breasts or genitals forcibly removed. The strappado involved tying the hands behind the back before the victim was raised by the wrists on a pulley and jerked, often with weights attached to the feet. The pear of anguish, a pear-shaped metal object, would be inserted into an orifice. It would then be unscrewed so that it opened out and expanded to cause extreme pain and mutilation.

Most punishments relied on a form of crushing.

The Psychology behind the Persecutions

It is estimated that the witch craze or 'The Burning Time' that swept Europe in the sixteenth and seventeenth centuries resulted in forty thousand deaths. This attitude towards witchcraft was very different to that of earlier times. During the Middle Ages, witches were seen as deluded old women. These wise-women, cunning folk or common sorcerers were, in the main, tolerated. Many scholars have tried to identify the factors that generated the change in attitude but the psychology behind witch hunts is still not fully understood. None of the theories account for regional variations or explain why some misfortunes were blamed on witchcraft whilst others were not. It is generally agreed that the upsurge in witchcraft accusations under the Tudors and Stuarts was a symptom of profound social change. It is an age-old human reaction to seek a scapegoat in times of turmoil and when change seems to be spiralling out of control. As Gaskill wrote, 'our ancestors were mostly decent and intelligent people who could sink to the worst cruelty and credulity at times of intense anxiety'.[5]

A widely held belief is that the witch craze was a product of religious extremism. Prior to the Reformation, Catholicism allowed believers the hope of salvation through good works, confession and absolution. Calvanistic theories of predestination were

---

5 Gaskill, Malcolm. *Witchfinders: a seventeenth century English tragedy,* 2005, John Murray, p. xv.

less comforting; if ones fate was predestined then one might just as well sell ones soul to the devil. The Protestant reformers viewed the devil as a continued threat. The tolerant attitude towards the cunning folk of the Middle Ages was no longer possible in an era when magic was regarded as only being possible with the assistance of the devil. The political power of the church in Europe at this time meant that heresy and treason were inextricably linked.

There is some suggestion that the upsurge in Puritanism led to increased persecutions and that witches were more likely to be Catholic. This could account for regional variations, with more persecutions taking place in areas where Puritanism held sway. For the Puritans, idleness was a sin and this may have made Puritans less likely to offer charity to supplicants. Although religious turmoil was a factor that created an atmosphere in which witch persecutions could flourish, the link

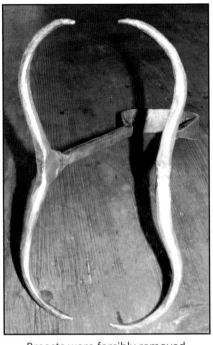

Breasts were forcibly removed.

with Puritanism is an oversimplification and does not stand up to scrutiny. Alongside this was the, largely unfounded, suggestion that witchcraft was associated with the Royalist cause, whereas the persecutors tended to be Parliamentarian.

It must be remembered that the witch craze took place against a background of a rising population and increasing poverty. This, as much as Puritan beliefs, led to a hardening of attitudes. It maybe that those who refused to give alms felt more comfortable if they could justify their lack of charity by regarding the applicant as a witch. Although, by the seventeenth century, the Elizabethan Poor Law had created some form of structured provision for the poor, political upheavals and civil war meant that prices rose whilst levels of relief remained the same.

The accusatorial judicial system of the early Middle Ages, with its focus on trial by ordeal, was less suited to witch hunts than the later, evidence based, inquisitorial system, where statements were collected and witnesses cross-examined. Yet it was this same legal system, coupled with changes in ideology and the weakening power of the church, which led to the decline in the number of persecutions, as the reliability of the evidence began to be questioned. Thus, by the end of the seventeenth century, witchcraft was no longer a capital offence.

Known Indictments

Essex 473, Kent 132, Hertfordshire 71, Surrey 33, Middlesex 63

What was this ideological change that brought an end to the witch hunts? Renaissance philosophers saw the work of the magus, the learned magician, as commensurate with humanist beliefs. They viewed magic as a natural science, without demonic associations.

There were those, like Reginald Scot,[6] who railed against witchcraft persecutions and believed that those who considered themselves to be witches were mentally ill however this remained a minority view until the eighteenth century. Underpinning a belief in witchcraft is the concept of ill-wishing; the assumption that one person can cause evil to another remotely. Renaissance thought and the changes wrought by the Reformation cast doubts upon this premis. Macfarlane cites 'less collectivist religion, a market economy, greater social mobility, and a growing separation of people through the formation of institutional rather than personal ties',[7] as reasons why intellectual beliefs in witchcraft were no longer possible.

Were there indeed witchcraft cults in seventeenth century Britain or was there just a conspiracy theory? There is little evidence that cults actually existed but what is

6   He published *The Discoverie of Witchcraft* in 1584.
7   MacFarlane, Alan. *Witchcraft in Tudor and Stuart England: a regional and comparative study*, 1970, Routledge p. 202.

important is the universal belief in witchcraft that prevailed. For our ancestors, it mattered not whether witchcraft persecutions were fuelled by religious, economic or political upheaval. Or if they were a product of urbanisation, increased literacy or changing attitudes to women; all of which theories have been mooted.[8] In order to understand our seventeenth century ancestors, we need to be aware that 'villagers were constantly engaged in contending with, or discussing, witches.'[9] This was a climate in which mass hysteria could easily tip the balance and create an atmosphere where our ancestors would become either accuser or accused.

Further Reading

Davies, Owen. *Cunning Folk: Popular Magic in English History,* 2007, Hambledon Continuum.

Gaskill, Malcolm. *Witchfinders: a seventeenth century English tragedy,* 2005, John Murray.

MacFarlane, Alan. *Witchcraft in Tudor and Stuart England: a regional and comparative study,* 1970, Routledge.

Martin, Lois *The History of Witchcraft,* 2007. Pocket Essentials.

Maxwell-Stuart, P.G. *Witchcraft a History,* 2000, Tempus Publishing Ltd.

Maxwell-Stuart, P.G. *Witch Hunters,* 2005, Tempus Publishing Ltd.

Merrifield, Ralph. *The Archaeology of Ritual and Magic,* 1987, Batsford.

Merrifield, Ralph. 'The Use of Bellarmines as Witch-Bottles' in *Guildhall Miscellany* 3, February 1954, offprint.

Sharpe, James. *Instruments of Darkness: Witchcraft in Early Modern England,* 1997, University of Pennsylvania Press.

<<**www.witchtrials.co.uk**>> Although this site is ostensibly about the Essex witch trials, it contains a great deal of general information including details of the witchcraft acts and a long list of those tried by witchcraft all over England.

<<**www.nationalgeographic.com/salem**>> The Salem witch trials.

<<**www.karisgarden.co.uk/cunningfolk/**>> Cunning Folk.

---

8   See, for example, Evans-Pritchard in MacFarlane, Alan. *Witchcraft in Tudor and Stuart England: a regional and comparative study,* 1970, Routledge, p. xxvii.

9   MacFarlane, Alan. *Witchcraft in Tudor and Stuart England: a regional and comparative study,* 1970, Routledge, p. 113.

CHAPTER 10

Horn-books, Hautebois, Hokeys and Hoops: childhood, pastimes and festivals

Childbirth

Although childbearing and childrearing did not warrant attention in Gervase Markham's *'The English Housewife'*, there was help for expectant and new mothers in the seventeenth century. In 1671, Jane Sharpe wrote *'The Midwives' Book: or, the whole art of midwifry discovered'*, later published as *'The Compleat Midwives' Companion'*. This was an expensive, illustrated book, aimed at the middle classes. It gave advice to those assisting at births and also covered such topics as conception, miscarriage and breast feeding. Antenatal care was rudimentary and might consist of taking cinnamon, which was thought to bring forth lusty children.

The lying-in room was kept warm and dark and was not necessarily the sleeping chamber. Women were unlikely to give birth in bed. Instead, a squatting or kneeling position would be assumed and a birthing-chair might be used. With the exception of the few male midwives, men were rarely present at a delivery. The mother was assisted by close women friends or relatives. These were known as her gossips, or god-sibs, the origin of god-parents. The gossips were responsible for making a nourishing spiced ale, or caudle, for the mother. Religion and superstition played a significant part in the day to day lives of our Stuart ancestors. The fear of childbirth

---

A Test for Barrenness

Take some small quantities of barley or any other corn that will soon grow, and soak part of it in the man's urine and part of it in the woman's urine, for a whole day and a night. Then take the corn out of the urine and lay them apart upon some floor, or in parts where it may dry, and in every morning water them both with their own urine and so continue. That corn that grows first is the most fruitful, and so is the person whose urine was the cause of it.

From Jane Sharpe's *The Midwives' Book*

---

meant that women relied heavily on prayers or amulets, or both, at this time. The churching of women, whereby new mothers attended a special church service shortly after birth, was still being practiced in the seventeenth century. It was a ceremony that was seen to have Catholic overtones and was therefore frowned upon by the Puritans.

Some middle aged women, who had had several children of their own, would gain a reputation for being an asset during deliveries and became the uno- fficial village midwife, although there were also licensed midwives. Profes- sional medical help was usually only sought when the labour proved par- ticularly difficult; by which time the mother was probably beyond all aid. The cost of this form of assistance was prohibitive for most families. Various herbal remedies might be used during labour, aquilegia and fennel both being recommended but there was little that could be done if the delivery was not

From the *Compleat Midwives' Companion*.

straightforward. Forceps were invented, by the Huguenot surgeon Peter Chamberlen, in the seventeenth century but they remained a closely guarded family secret for the next hundred years. His nephew, also Peter Chamberlen, attended the birth of the future Charles II. Caesareans were known but were normally reserved for removing a child from a dead mother, as the resulting blood loss made the chance of maternal survival very remote.

It is thought likely that 5-10% of all births led to the death of the mother. The most frequent cause was puerperal infection, brought on by the lack of cleanliness of the birth attendants or their instruments. There was no understanding of the need for hygiene or the sterilisation of instruments until the nineteenth century. As most married women gave birth at least six times, producing a family was a high risk activity.

Wet nurses might be hired by middle class families, or in cases where the mother had died, or was unable to feed the baby herself. Hannah Wolley's guidance for wet nurses gives specific instructions that they should abstain from spicy foods, take moderate exercise and refrain from copulation because 'it retracts, diminishes, and makes her milk to be an unsavoury taste, rendering it hot, rank or goatish, which is very prejudicial to the infant.'[1] Although breast feeding normally continued well into

---

1   Wolley, Hannah. *The Compleat Servant-maid: or, the young maiden's and family's daily companion*, 2010, Gale ECCO Print, (9th edition 1719), p. 8.

Advice for the Dry Nurse

Do not terrify {children} into complyence by talking of ghost, spirits, hobgoblins, and such like ridiculous things (which is a wicked method too often put in practice to the great detriment of children) for, comparatively speaking, they are as soft as wax. The first impression will be deep, and as they increase in years, they will retain it stronger, and it will be almost impossible ever to root it out of their minds. This evil and unhappy method of proceeding has cow'd and ruined many promising and hopeful spirits, and when people have imbibed these fallacious and dangerous notions in their infancy, and persevered therein till they have arrived to maturity, they have become dull, heavy and ridiculous in their more advanced years.

From Hannah Wolley's *Compleat Servant-maid*

the second year of life, some solid food was often introduced fairly early on. Bread and milk, known as pap, was recommended and bran was also given to small babies. Honey, or powdered coral in milk, were regarded as important in the prevention of fits. Teething rings of coral, ivory or silver would be for the rich but bone was substituted in poorer households. Much of Hannah Wolley's advice does not sound out of place in modern times. She advocated swaddling, guarding against favouritism and praise rather than threats.

Toys

Childhood was fairly restricted in the 1600s and most children were mini-adults, taking on tasks that contributed to the household as soon as they were able. Even in wealthy families, there was little opportunity for play. Toys were usually home-made, often from wood, or might be adapted from household objects. The metal rings that held the staves of barrels together became hoops and the laundry beetle became a bat. With the addition of a cock, a bat could be used to play paddy-whack, or paddle-whack. The cock, a cork with feathers inserted, was so called because it was thought to resemble a cockerel. This had to be hit successively without letting it fall to the floor, each hit scoring another point. Battledore, a forerunner of badminton that used similar equipment, required the shuttlecock to be hit from player to player.

Nine-men's morris[2] and five stones, later known as jacks, required very little

---

2 This is not dissimilar to naughts and crosses. Two players take it in turns to place one of their nine 'men', usually stones, on a grid, which could be drawn on the earth. The first to place three men in a row was the winner.

equipment. Basic woodworking skills could produce a top or a bilbo. The latter was a wooden cup, attached by string to a wooden ball. The aim was to swing the ball and get it to land in the cup. Quoits were played, not just by throwing rings over a pole on the ground but also by each player each holding a stick and throwing the rings from one to another. Dolls could be made in the home from cloth or wood. Wooden dolls were known as Bartholomew babies, because they were sold at the St Bartholomew's Day Fair, which was held every August in Smithfield, London. Solitaire boards could also be hand made but the, more elaborate, chess sets were for the rich.

Toys were usually home-made from wood.

Like their modern counterparts, Stuart children would have appreciated certain foodstuffs as special treats. Comfits, crystallised fruits or flower petals, would be prized but the sugar content made them a luxury. The only sweet that would still be recognisable today was barley sugar, which came from France during the seventeenth century. Although barley sugar did contain barley water, as well as sugar and cream of tartar, the name probably came from the French, sucre brule, or burnt sugar.

Very few children would have had access to books and any that were written with children in mind were highly moral in tone and intended to educate and not entertain. The works

A Bilbo was a wooden cup, attached by string to a ball.

of John Bunyan come into this category. As well as his better known *'Pilgrim's Progress'* Bunyan wrote *'A Book for Boys and Girls, or Country Rhimes for Children'*[3] which contained verses aimed at teaching children the ten commandments.

This was a time when formal employment was likely to have begun by the age of twelve; following several years of work within the family. Days that provided the opportunity for play and enjoyment would therefore be the exception, rather than the rule, for children of the Stuart era.

Schooling

Seventeenth century schooling was the preserve of the better off and was almost exclusively aimed at males. Boys might be taught to read, although not necessarily write, in petty schools, whereas grammar schools would provide a more rounded education, based on mathematics, scripture, logic, Latin, Greek and Hebrew. The

---

3   Later editions were entitled *'Divine Emblems, or Temporal Things Spiritualized'*.

school day was long, starting as early as 6.00am in summer and continuing until 6.00pm, with a two hour break for lunch. Younger pupils were taught by the usher, whilst the headmaster was responsible for the older boys. The wealthiest families would be more likely to employ a private tutor for their sons. In the absence of formal teacher training, the local clergy or household chaplains were frequently pressed into service as educators. Charity schools, such as the Bluecoats foundations, did allow for the education of some poorer children.

It is difficult to assess levels of literacy in the 1600s. It seems likely that about 30% of the population could read to some extent and that this may have risen to 50% by the end of the century. Undoubtedly, literacy rates were higher in the cities, such as London and Bristol and more men could read than women. It is difficult enough to gather reliable evidence that arrives at these figures and assessing how *well* individuals could read is next to impossible. Those who could struggle through printed books might not be able to read handwriting, particularly that produced by someone who was themselves not very proficient. The Puritan influence meant that studying the Bible was regarded as a virtue and reading was encouraged for this purpose. The more affluent housewife was also expected to be able to read and keep basic household accounts; skills which she would have learnt at home. Any further academic education for girls was normally viewed as being unnecessary. A few boarding schools, for girls of wealthy families did exist, mostly in London. There the young women followed a very different curriculum from their brothers, with accomplishments such as music, French or fine needlework being taught.

The earliest known, illustrated alphabet book, *'The Childes First Tutor: or, the master and mistris'*, was published in 1664. For most children, reading was learnt from a horn book. This was a hand-held wooden object with the alphabet and Lord's prayer written on parchment, which was covered with a thin piece of horn for protection. Those who were learning to write would practice extensively on a slate before they were allowed to try pen and ink. Ink could be made from oak apples and quill pens

Reading was learnt from a horn-book.

were made from goose or swans' feathers. Vellum, parchment and paper were all written on. When using vellum, pounce was also needed. This was ground cuttlefish bone or pumice, which was rubbed into the vellum so that it became less greasy and the ink could penetrate. The writer could choose the smoother inside of the skin or the outer side, which although less greasy was rougher because of the animal hair.

English university education meant Oxford or Cambridge, although some English boys went to Scottish or European universities. It is thought that there were nearly two thousand students at Cambridge alone at the dawn of the seventeenth century. Many of these young men would be destined for the church or the law. Some would become physicians but others were seeking a broader education before taking up the life of a landed gentleman.

The new theories of the Renaissance were very slow to permeate the university curriculum; learning was still traditional, with an emphasis on Aristotelian ideas. Teaching took the form of hour long lectures, which began at 7.00am. These might be held in public, or privately in the dining room, chapel or tutor's rooms. The students displayed their knowledge through disputations, or structured debates, with their fellow students and tutors. They were also required to give presentations known as declamations, peppered with quotations from the Greek and Latin classics. Subjects included physics, mathematics, medicine, rhetoric, philosophy, ethics, astronomy and music. Rhetoric, defined as the art of eloquent communication, embraced history, literature and scripture.

The concept of the need for an academic education would be foreign to the majority of our seventeenth century ancestors. In order to equip themselves for their daily lives, they would however have to acquire many practical skills and these would be passed on within the family or in some cases, through an apprenticeship.

Leisure Pursuits

Like their children, most seventeenth century adults lacked the time for leisure pursuits. Sundays were the only days on which our labouring ancestors were comparatively free from work. The religious climate dictated that, on that day, only the essential household and farm jobs, such as the feeding of livestock, could be done. Attendance at church might be the only weekly event that did not constitute work and most social activities centred round the church. Once the obligatory church service was over however there was little else on offer. Even walking for pleasure on a Sunday was forbidden under Puritan rule; only going to and from church was allowed.

Sports such as bear-baiting, cock fighting and horse racing were popular with those who could afford it. As these activities were normally accompanied by betting, drinking and riotous behaviour, they were frowned upon by the Puritans and banned during the

Archery was a sport available to our seventeenth century ancestors.

reign of Charles I. Soldiers attempted to regulate these activities by destroying the animals involved. The seventeenth century was the heyday of real tennis. Promoted by Charles I, it was described as the sport of kings but the working man would have lacked the resources, energy or time for such activities. The long-bow was no longer used in warfare; Elizabeth I having abandoned it, in favour of weapons of fire, in the 1590s. Archery was therefore available to our seventeenth century ancestors as a sport, rather than an activity that had to be practiced for military purposes.

There were ball games that could be accessed by the lower classes. Camp ball was Medieval in origin and known by various other names, including, cnapan in Wales. This was a rowdy team game, where the ball passed from hand to hand on a playing area that could include the whole village. Despite Oliver Cromwell being described as 'more famous for his exercises in the fields than in the schools …being one of the chief matchmakers and players of football',[4] this was another sport that was considered to be inappropriate, particularly on a Sunday.

One thing that was regarded as being open to most classes was the theatre. This would be an option for our London ancestors only. In the provinces, touring companies, sponsored by the nobility, might act in the homes of their patrons. Fear of social unrest and plague saw the theatres close in 1642. They did not re-open until after the Restoration in 1660 and from this time, women began to act in theatres. For

---

4   Heath, James. *Flagellum: or the life and death, birth and burial of Oliver Cromwell,* 1665, Randall Taylor, p.8.

Description of the Ball Game, Cnapan

About one or two of the clock afternoon begins the play, in this sort, after a cry made both parties draw to into some plain, all first stripped bare saving a light pair of breeches, bare-headed, bare-bodied, bare legs and feet.... There is a round ball prepared of a reasonable quantity so as a man may hold it in his hand and no more, this ball is of some massy wood as box, yew, crab or holly tree and should be boiled in tallow to make it slippery and hard to hold. This ball is called cnapan and is by one of the company hurling bolt upright into the air, and at the fall he that catches it hurls it towards the country he plays for, for goal or appointed place there is none neither needs any, for the play is not given over until the cnapan be so far carried that there is no hope to return it back that night, for the carrying of it a mile or two miles from the first place is no losing of the honour so it be still followed by the company and the play still maintained, it is oftentimes seen the chase to follow two miles and more.

From George Owen's *The Description of Pembrokeshire 1603*

most of our seventeenth century relatives, the only performances they would see would be the occasional mystery or morality play, which lingered on from Medieval times. These often took the form of tableaux, displayed during a procession, or they might be performed in town inn-yards.

Music was another pastime of the 1600s, although the more elaborate instruments, such as harpsichords and hautbois, an early form of oboe, would have been beyond the budget of ordinary families. Lutes, viols and flutes were also popular. The style of classical music normally associated with the seventeenth century is Baroque, with composers such as Lully, Pachelbel and Purcell being prominent. It is unlikely that most of our Stuart ancestors would have been familiar with this music. Instead they would make their own music, playing folk dances and local tunes. A simple wooden pipe or a tabor, which was a small, hand-held drum, might be used, as these could be home-made, though stringed instruments were also found in some less affluent households.

Indoor games for adults included backgammon, chess and draughts. Dice and cards were also played but these too attracted disapproval and were banned. Despite the censure of the authorities, betting and games of chance were popular. A man might

A man might challenge all-comers to remove the ring from the chains joining two horseshoes.

attempt to win the price of his beer in the alehouse on the roll of a dice, or by challenging all-comers to remove a ring from the chains joining two horseshoes.

With such a limited range of pastimes and social events available to ordinary folk, it is not surprising that fairs, festivals and holidays were eagerly anticipated.

High Days and Holydays

Even weekly market days gave our ancestors a break from routine. The village and town fairs, that were held two or three times a year, offered a greater opportunity for relaxation, as well as trading and job seeking. It was also a chance to meet friends and prospective spouses. Apart from stalls selling both essential and more luxurious items, there might be competitions and side shows, followed by a bonfire and dancing.

Most annual festivals had pagan origins, even if they had been adopted by the Christian church. May-day and midsummer celebrations were out of favour with the Puritans because of their secular undertones. May-day festivities included the maypole, which was seen to have sexual connotations, so May-day observance was banned in 1644. The ancient tradition of lighting midsummer fires for protection on the summer solstice, June the 23rd, had been discredited during the Reformation. Nonetheless, in the 1600s, many rural communities still celebrated midsummer by decorating their homes with garlands and holding public bonfires and feasts.

By the seventeenth century, the celebration of the successful gathering of the harvest in September or October had replaced the earlier commemoration of Lammas Day. This took the form of the harvest hokey, held by local farmers for their workers. Feasting, music and dancing would mark the end of the busiest period of the agricultural year. Harvest festivals did not become part of the church calendar until 1843.

The celebration of Christmas, for those who could afford it, saw a period of twelve days' feasting. This was an ideal opportunity to make use of any produce that would not keep through the winter. Goose or beef, rather than turkey, would be the meat of choice and there would be extravagant use of dried fruits. The Yule log adorned the hearth and houses would be decorated with evergreens, symbols of life to anticipate the return of spring. Carols, or curls, were sung. These were often regional in nature and might be performed on Christmas Eve by the local Waits, who would go from house to house to sing.

Wassailing was a custom that was long associated with Christmas. Wassail comes from the Saxon greeting 'waes hael', or 'be well'. The response, 'drink hail', means 'drink and be healthy'. Wassailers would travel from house to house, wishing their neighbours well and hoping that cake and ale would be distributed. This was often a practice reserved for Twelfth Night. A traditional wassail brew, especially in the west country, was Lamb's Wool, a corruption of 'La mas ubal' or apple fruit day. This was made from warmed ale or cider, sugar and roasted apples or crab apples; spices and cream might be added. Commonly, in cider producing areas, wassailing, or apple howling, also formed part of a ceremony to keep evil spirits from the orchards during the following year. A rowdy procession would follow the apple king and queen from orchard to orchard blessing the trees. This was accompanied by shouting, the banging of drums and muskets being fired over the tops of the trees.

A Harvest Song

Merry, merry, merry, cheary, cheary, cheary,
Trowle the black bowle to me ;
Hey derry, derry, with a poupe and a lerry,
Ile trowle it againe to thee:
Hooky, hooky, we have shorne,
And we have bound,
And we have brought Harvest
Home to towne.

From Thomas Nashe's *Summer's Last Will and Testament 1600*

Twelfth Night Celebrations

Thence, after play ... (there being acted the Tempest) ... home where we find my house with good fires and candles ready ... and so with much pleasure we fell to dancing, having extraordinary music, two violins and a bass viallin and theorbo (four hands) ... a very good supper and mighty merry and good music playing; and after supper to dancing and singing until about 12 at night; and then we had a good sack-posset for them and an excellent cake.

From Samuel Pepys' *Diary 1667/8*

The very name, Christ-*mass*, had Catholic overtones and for this reason, the Puritans wanted to rename it Christ-tide and mark it only by fasting and prayer. A directive of January 1644/5 stated that only Sundays were to be regarded as holy days and that all other 'festival days, vulgarly called Holy Days, having no warrant in the Word of God, are not to be continued'. Mince pies, which were at this time filled with meat and rosewater, were traditionally an oval shape, to resemble Christ's manger. This led to them being outlawed as idolatrous. Parliamentarian soldiers attempted to enforce the ban on Christmas celebrations by confiscating festive food and removing decorations. This prohibition was reiterated in an ordinance of June 1647, which also attempted to establish the second Tuesday of each month as a secular holiday to give workers a break. In the 1650s, more legislation forbade Christmas services from being held on the 25th of December and businesses were expected to open as usual. What people did in their own homes largely went unnoticed but there was some public defiance to the ban. In Canterbury, what became known as the Plum Pudding Riots broke out. Market traders refused to open on Christmas Day and instead played a mammoth ball game[5] with thousands of participants, calling for the return of Christmas or the restoration of the monarchy. Christmas celebrations resumed under Charles II but they were not as lavish as those of the first half of the century.

From John Taylor's *The Vindication of Christmas*.

---

5   Possibly football or camp ball.

In the seventeenth century, childhood was all too brief and time for enjoyment was limited. For adults and children alike, breaks in the monotony of daily life would have been welcomed and enjoyed to the full. If a will mentions a musical instrument or a book, we may catch a glimpse of how our ancestors spent their leisure time. In the absence of such details we can only imagine them participating in the feasts, fairs and festivals that were part of the seasonal cycle in their locality.

Further Reading
Baines, Anthony. *Victoria and Albert Museum: catalogue of musical instruments, Vol. II,* 1968, HMSO.

Costello, William T. *The Scholastic Curriculum at early Seventeenth Century Cambridge,* 1958, Oxford University Press.

Cressy, David. *Literacy and the Social Order: reading and writing in Tudor and Stuart England,* 2006, Cambridge University Press.

Hobby Elaine [ed.] Raynalde, Thomas. *The Birth of Mankind: otherwise named the woman's book,* 2009, Ashgate, (1540).

Hobby, Elaine [ed.] Sharp, Jane. *The Midwives' Book or, the whole art of Midwifry Discovered,* 1999, Oxford University Press, (1671).

Hutton, Ronald. *The Rise and Fall of Merry England: the ritual year 1400-1700,* 1994, Oxford University Press.

Russell, Raymond. *Victoria and Albert Museum: catalogue of musical instruments, Vol. I,* 1968, HMSO.

Thomas, Ian [ed.] Culpeper, Nicholas. *Book of Birth; a seventeenth century guide to having lusty children,* 1985, Webb and Bower, (1651).

Wolley, Hannah. *The Compleat Servant-maid: or, the young maiden's and family's daily companion,* 2010, Gale ECCO Print, (9th edition 1719).[6]

---

6   The first edition appeared in 1677.

Index